P r ɑ

"Everything just

Introducing the d

Results has made me far more productive inside and outside of work. I use it daily to manage my time and my relationships. When expectations are clear and unquestionable, it is imperative that you monitor the results to make sure the expectations are accomplished. Otherwise, why spend the time setting the expectation? It works and it is easy to execute."

– Louis M. Centolella III, Vice President, Sales
Ontario Credit Corporation / Computer Gallery

"Students, teachers and administrators would benefit greatly from *Mouth Off*, because they would have to take ownership instead of always pointing the finger."

– Marie Korta, retired teacher

"Anyone in a sales or management position should read this book. Chuck shares his concepts in a simple, straight forward in your face manner that will get you thinking. Give this book two hours and it will change the way you do business!"

– Peter L. Derrenbacker CLU, ChFC, CFP
Northwestern Mutual Financial Network

"*Mouth Off* is a thought provoking how-to book about developing a customer-focused Corporate Culture. It lays out a step by step methodology for both Management and Sales Staff to follow. Most importantly it is easy to implement and provides a simple way to monitor results. I sincerely recommend this book to anyone interested in ensuring they stay 'customer focused.'"

–Ken Henson Jr.
Corporate Director, Chief Information Officer

"Thank you so much for sharing a pre-publication copy of your wonderful book with me! *Mouth Off* is refreshing in its candor and practicality. It's not often that an author truly delivers upon a promise − 'I'm going to show you how to become a stronger, more decisive leader' − you do just that."

− Debbie Sydow, President
Onondaga Community College

"Wait a minute! What do Bill Cosby, General George S. Patton, Vince Lombardi, and some guy that makes omelets have to do with my sales career? After reading *Mouth Off*, the answer is A LOT! Chuck has a unique and refreshing approach to define and break down the components of successful selling. From rookie salesman to seasoned veteran, chapter after chapter of this thought provoking, insightful book will add to your sales arsenal. As a multiple award winning sales representative for a dealership, selling products for the world's largest construction machinery manufacturer, my advice is − read this book before your competition does!"

− Nick Copanas, Heavy Equipment Sales Specialist
Milton CAT

"I just finished reading *Mouth Off*, written by Chuck Togias. Eighteen years ago I was the #1 top sales professional for the #1 Minolta business equipment dealer in the United States. I then met Chuck Togias and had the privilege to hear him speak to our company and soon after that day my sales literally doubled. Even better, my relationships in business became stronger, my referral business jumped through the roof and I gained a mentor and a friend, named Chuck Togias. I am now the Executive Vice President of a successful investment firm and have been listening to and nurturing my clients for 13 years. Chuck Togias comes to work with me in some capacity every day."

− Alan D. Peck
Executive Vice President
Pinnacle Financial Group, LLC

by CHUCK
Togias

**When to talk,
when to listen
and how to succeed.**

For more information on the sales and leadership methods
found in this book, go to **Step2Training.net**

To order additional copies, please contact us.
BookSurge, LLC
www.booksurge.com
1-866-308-6235
orders@booksurge.com

Cover illustration and design by Ryan Mikesell

ACKNOWLEDGEMENTS

———

A book such as this could never be a one-man endeavor. There were many, many people who gave me the necessary nudges, encouragements and even occasional whacks on the head when needed. To each of you who contributed in some way to this piece, my sincerest thanks.

A few I'd like to mention by name.

To my editor and friend, Wally Stoneman, whose day job is as the Creative Director at an advertising agency – I could not have completed this project without you. Your patience, work ethic and great attitude are incredible. You are an invaluable resource to any company or project, especially this one. Words cannot express my appreciation.

And, of course, a special thanks to my wife Linda, whose support for this project from the very beginning, as well as ongoing encouragement throughout the tedious process, was essential in this book seeing the light of day. Her undying love and continued dedication make life wonderful. Plus, she's the only person I know who can truly get away with telling me when to turn *my* mouth off.

TABLE OF CONTENTS

FOREWORD

——

My background in accounting afforded me the opportunity to be involved in the overall depths of the corporate structure. The financial requirements and all the concerns of business have always been my responsibility. Many financial people or people who have no direct contact with the customer do not understand the importance of the customer. They view the customer as a fact or line on a financial statement. In order to be an effective and successful enterprise, the focus has to be beyond the numbers and to the warm bodies that make up the numbers. My philosophy has always been that everyone in the company is in sales. It doesn't matter what role a person takes in the corporate structure, it only matters what attitude that person accepts and understands while that person functions in that role. Chuck Togias has a business philosophy that parallels my personal beliefs. In reading this book, it not only confirms the importance of a strong customer-focused environment, but also projects the plan to facilitate the philosophy. During my personal experiences of thirty-five plus years as Chief Financial Officer and Vice President, our company experienced a continual fourteen percent growth rate per year when following the practices similar to those expressed in this book. Our continual attention to the customer's needs and the concerted effort to deliver quality products at competitive prices insured the continual growth.

I have always said that sales cure a lot of ills. Continual sales and repeat sales sustain a company. From the depths of the company to the most outer limits of the company, Chuck Togias' messages are strong and direct. Everyone is involved in making it happen for the customer, the company and each other. Sales are an accumulated effort of all in order to super serve the customer. Strength is in the ability to solve problems more than the ability to close the sale. When emphasis is placed on solving problems relating to the needs, strong trust bonds are built between customer and company. Price objections melt in the presence of great ideas.

An uncle of mine, who was very successful in business, had a saying: *"If we could give everyone a 'common sense' pill every morning, business, government and people would function more efficiently and the world would be a better and more peaceful place."* This book is clear, concise and powerful. As I mentioned, my background is accounting and the numbers that make up the success or failure of a business. It is much easier to accept good financial news than bad. Applying a straightforward common sense philosophy to a business, as illustrated in this book, generates a greater opportunity for that business to deliver positive results to the bottom line. We all know that the bottom line speaks for itself in delivering benefits to the owners, managers, staff and especially the customers. Customers also are naturally drawn to successful businesses.

The interest, application and lasting benefits of this book will leave the reader with a greater understanding of what a successful business is all about. It not only fulfills needs, but lays out the formula for competitive success that applies to any business.

-- Ralph Rimualdo, CCE
Former VP, CFO of Case Supply

PREFACE

———

You've probably read a ton of sales books, and I'm sure you picked up a few good tips from each. But essentially, they've all said the same thing. Until now.

I assure you, you've never read a sales book like this. For one thing, it's packed with a ton of useful, provocative leadership lessons you just won't find in a typical sales and self-help book. For another, instead of relying on the typical business analogies found in most of these books, I'm going to draw my analogies from areas that *everyone* can relate to: the flaws in our country's judicial and political systems, and the lack of leadership in our homes, schools and community at large. Strong stuff? You bet. I told you you've never read anything like it.

Of course, at its core this book is designed to make you a better sales professional. It's based on my Step2 Training System and my view of life. Along the way I hope to make you think. Make you question. Make you doubt. And make you mad. In the end, this will all serve to make you a strong leader – not only at work but in every other aspect of your life.

Now, about the title: *Mouth Off*. Appropriate, because before we get to our core lessons, I'm going to rant a bit about things that, on the surface, are not related to sales. Like the lack of leadership in this country. The failings of the judicial and political systems. And the dangers of idol worship. Then I'll show you how studying the shortfalls of these systems – and then doing the exact opposite of what they do – will greatly improve your chances of success.

The other side of *Mouth Off* is about learning when to do just that – turn your mouth off so you can listen. When used properly, this not-so-secret weapon will drive your results through the roof.

Oh, and something else you should probably know: I have very strong opinions. About everything. That's why the cover of this book is all black and white with only a hint of red. Black and white, because that's how I see the world. Something's either wrong or it's right. Period. And red, because that's what I see every time I hear of people who constantly hang out in the gray area. Man they make me mad. Unfortunately, they also make up a majority of society. And to me, that's the major reason for many of the ills in our society today. Everyone's afraid to take a stand that's not politically correct. Everyone wants to be wishy-washy and stay in the middle where it's safe. *If you don't stand for something, you stand for nothing.*

If my strong opinions offend you, good. Breaking out of your comfort zone is a key component to growth – both professionally as well as personally. And make no mistake – if you apply the lessons in this book, *you will become more successful.* If you don't, if you faithfully apply these rules and you don't improve your results, *I will buy this book back from you.* How's that for a strong opinion.

So here's the deal: I'm going to tell you what's wrong with leadership in this country and give you some real-world examples for proof. Then I'm going to show you how to become a stronger, more decisive leader yourself. And in the process I'm going to introduce you to some ordinary folks who, through their ability to listen, communicate and build relationships, became extraordinarily successful. And finally, I'm going to introduce you to my unique, customer-focused Step2 system that helps you use all of these lessons to achieve measurable results.

So find a comfortable chair. Put your feet up. Grab a high-lighter. And know that while you're sitting, I'll be taking a stand.

This is gonna be fun.

CHAPTER ONE

Leadership?
WHAT LEADERSHIP?

This is the chapter where I'm going to blast the leadership - or lack thereof - in this country.

But Chuck, isn't this a book about sales and personal development? Yes. But great salespeople, as well as great companies, are enhanced with strong effective leadership. Sometimes, the best way to learn *how* to do something is to learn how *not* to do it. The examples in this chapter are definitely how *not* to do it.

So who are you that you can be the defining authority on leadership? Well, for starters, I spent 30 years in sales and sales management, most of that time in the broadcast industry. Back in the late 70s, I became General Sales Manager of a radio station that, at the time, had a 17% revenue market share. Four years later, we had a 40% share. And six years after that, we had a 55% revenue share – in a 21-station market. How'd we do it? Through incredible teamwork propelled by focused, defined leadership.

I am also streetwise and intelligent, and I can spot the truth when I see it – and the lack of it just as easily. Come on, you do not need to be a PhD to get the point that we need better leaders. Our judicial and political leaders have compromised themselves and their institutions. They are no longer morally or ethically sound yet they defend their actions. I have been wrong many times on ethical and moral issues. The difference is I knew it, confronted it and eventually changed.

There's no shortage of leaders in this country. After all everywhere you turn, someone's being heralded as a leader of this or a leader of that. There are people heralded as "leaders in the black community," and those who are just plain old "community leaders." The term "civil rights leader" is thrown around rather loosely these days, as are the terms "corporate leader" and "church leader." So my question is, with so many so-called leaders running around, how come there's no leadership?

We'll find out in this chapter. We're going to take a look at the widespread lack of leadership in every aspect of life – from the home court to the Supreme Court – and try to discern why that lack of leadership persists.

I will use the Political System as an example of bad leadership and its results. The political system divides – it's become a system of blaming, finger-pointing and avoiding responsibility at all cost. Try that in business and see where it gets you.

I use the Judicial System as a great analogy of what happens when a salesman loses focus. The Judicial System compromises – it no longer focuses on finding the truth, it just tries to make sure procedures are adhered to. When a salesman likewise loses focus, and tries to sell products instead of solutions, the result is the same: loss of respect.

NOTE: It's important for you to know as you read on that I am not affiliated with either party - Republicans or Democrats. I am an Independent who votes according to the issues, not down some 'party line'. I believe that if a politician does not exhibit integrity, honor and leadership, he or she is not deserving of my support or respect, regardless of party. And let me tell you right now, ladies and gentlemen, there are VERY FEW politicians who have my respect.

Where have all the leaders gone?

A full 90% of our country's problems stem from weak leadership. Is that from a scientific study? No, it's my opinion. But I challenge you to try and prove me wrong. (I warned you I have strong opinions.) It starts with a lack of leadership in the home, carries over to the schools, community organizations, corporations, on up to the Federal Government. At every step of the way, people are afraid to stand for what's right. We've become so wishy-washy with our "moral relativism" that our value system is now built around doing everything in our power to not offend someone.

Let's look at the first link in this leadership chain: parents and the home. Time was, when your children acted up you disciplined them. This is what is referred to – almost nostalgically nowadays – as teaching children right from wrong. Whatever happened to 'spare the rod, spoil the child'? The most successful, well-adjusted adults I've ever met told me they came from very disciplined homes. As the writer of Proverbs tell us: "He who spares the rod hates his son, but he who loves him is careful to discipline him." *(Proverbs 13:24, New International Version).*

From *The Art of War*, Sun Tzu, the legendary Chinese general, we get this: "If, however, you are indulgent but unable to make your authority felt; kind hearted, but unable to enforce your commands; and incapable, moreover, of quelling disorder, then your soldiers should be likened to spoiled children; useless for any practical purpose."

It's gotten to the point where a complete stranger – a childless one at that – will call the police when they see a parent disciplining a screaming 3 year-old (pardon the redundancy) in a public place. Hmm. Not too hard to see where the leadership breakdown begins, is it?

Now let's look at the next link: the schools. Again, used to be that these hallowed halls were where children went to learn. What a quaint notion. And if one child was acting up in class and preventing the others from learning, that child was disciplined. Either by writing sentences (anybody remember that one?), being sent to the principal's office for a good paddling, or some other such punishment. What barbarians. Luckily, we live in an enlightened age where it's not about a child's education, per se, it's about their self esteem. And thanks to the upright, honorable Teachers Union, teachers are not judged based on how well they teach, but on how well they handle problems in the classroom. That's why our educational systems ranks 25th worldwide. What a disgrace with all our wealth and technical know-how. Our educational system is broke and no one wants to admit it or fix it. When children are not learning in school it is a direct reflection on teachers, administrators and the Teachers Union.

Here's where we jump straight to the Hall of Fame of Weak Leaders: Government. I'm lumping in city, state and federal "leaders" in this – from all political parties – because all are equally pathetic.

Whoa! Chuck, that's a strong word. Are you serious? You're calling our leaders pathetic?

Yes. Again, I challenge you to prove me wrong. Look at a few recent events (recent, at least, as of this writing.) In August of 2005, a terrible hurricane named Katrina hit the Southeast United States, with tragic results for many Gulf states. Perhaps worst hit, though, was the city of New Orleans. The high winds and raging waters caused by the hurricane ultimately caused a few of the city's levees to give way, flooding the storied city.

One would expect that during a tragic *natural disaster* such as this, people would be united in trying to help. The truth is, most average citizens were united in their offerings of help. But the leaders – those who are supposed to be helping unite us during such events – actually ended up being extremely divisive. When the poorest citizens of New Orleans found themselves stranded, and it took several days to bus them to safer areas, the finger-pointing began. Ray Nagin, the mayor of New Orleans, blamed the state and federal governments. Kathleen Babineaux Blanco, the governor of Louisiana, blamed the mayor and President Bush. Because the majority of the poor who live in the city are black, any delay in helping them was immediately labeled racism. As if the federal government's delay was not caused by lack of procedure (the feds *must* be asked by the governor of a state before providing assistance – state's rights you know), or logistics (the city was under water, not the easiest of environments to provide help), but rather was because the president and his advisers were sitting around saying, "Ah, what's the rush – they're just black folks."

Regardless of where you stand politically, you *cannot* believe that that was the case. It even got so bad that one of the famed Kennedy clan, Bobby Kennedy, Jr., blamed the president for the actual hurricane! His rationale had something to do with how global warming was the president's fault and that's what ultimately caused such a strong hurricane.

That, my friends, is not leadership.

Now I'm not defending the Federal Government in this event – they definitely made their share of mistakes – but at least they admitted that they could have handled things better. They tried to make changes, even went so far as to replace the head of FEMA, among other things. Yet to my knowledge, neither the Governor of Louisiana nor the mayor of New Orleans accepted any blame whatsoever in the handling of the evacuation and rescue attempts.

Great leaders do not divide. They always try to unite. When leaders divide, chaos results.

In October of the same year — just a few months after Katrina —

> **Great leaders do not divide. They unite.**

there was a terrible riot in Toledo, Ohio. Apparently, the National Socialist Movement — which promotes itself as America's Nazi Party — scheduled a march to protest black gangs' harassment of white residents. The march never took place due to the riots. People protesting the march vandalized buildings and set fire to a two-story building that housed a bar.

As warped as I think the Nazi's beliefs, and as misguided as I think they are, the bottom line is their planned march was a legal one. The violent response was not. The National Socialist Movement (NSM) was exercising their right to free speech. Those protesting them assumed they had some right to a violent reaction. Sadly, the so-called leaders of the community blamed the NSM for the violence, not the rioters. They absolved the rioters from breaking the law and vandalizing the neighborhood because they were "incited" to action by the vicious hate speech of the NSM.

If we had the "right" to react violently every time someone made a disparaging remark about us, we'd live in complete chaos. Fortunately, we have laws. Unfortunately, some of our leaders don't entirely respect them.

I sincerely believe most people do not discriminate against color; I believe, instead, that they discriminate against bad behavior. Especially when bad behavior is defended and justified by the leaders of a community.

Where, oh where, have our leaders gone?

Before you think I'm just some white guy taking easy shots at the black community, know this: to me, Martin Luther King, Jr. was a great leader. In fact, I firmly believe that if he were alive today, he would be considered one of the greatest leaders of all time. King was a strong leader with a sweet spirit. And, importantly, he got people to change. Under his leadership, people got better, not worse. Communities got better, not worse. King knew that the country had to change, but first the people had to change. He never blamed others. He always looked to solve the issues facing him in positive ways. Just imagine how the current so-called "leaders" of the black community would compare – or fail to compare – to MLK if he were alive today. Truth be told, I don't think most of our "leaders" today – regardless of color – could compare to our great leaders of the past. For instance, Dr. King, Abraham Lincoln, Franklin Delano Roosevelt, Vince Lombardi, John F. Kennedy and Ronald Reagan all put great emphasis on personal achievement and responsibility. And all were great leaders — because they made people accountable for their actions. As JFK challenged: "Ask not what your country can do for you, but ask what you can do for your country."

When everyone is accepted regardless of their behavior, top performance is jeopardized. It's like giving the poor performing students the same grade as the over achiever — a sure-fire way to sap the strength and enthusiasm from the top performers. That's why I have always liked to pay commission. It rewards performance.

There's a quote by Vince Lombardi that voices my sentiments exactly:

> "It is becoming increasingly difficult to be tolerant of a society who has sympathy only for the misfits, only for the maladjusted, only for the criminal, only for the loser. Have sympathy for them, help them but I think it's also a time for all of us to stand up for and to cheer for the doer, the achiever, one who recognizes a problem and does something about it, one who looks at something extra to do for his country, the winner, the leader!"

Now *that's* leadership.

Take a look at our war with Iraq. Were we justified in going over there? In my opinion, absolutely. No sane person would doubt that Saddam Hussein was a dangerous dictator. He repeatedly violated U.N. sanctions, murdered his own people mercilessly, and constantly violated human rights. From a human rights perspective we were completely justified in going.

Would I have actually sent troops? Absolutely not. Not with our pathetic political situation. We are too divided as a country to entertain going to war with any country at any time. We'll only end up looking weak because we have no resolve and won't carry through. Any war right now – with the sad state of our political system – would just be a big waste of money and an even bigger waste of life. The party seeking power will only have additional ammunition to divide our country even further. It's because of this divisiveness and lack of leadership that I'm a complete isolationist. Does that make you mad? Don't yell at me. Take it up with the mouthpieces in the Beltway. Until we can stand together as a country, we should leave the world's trouble spots to the U.N.

This division among our political leaders along party lines can almost be considered subversive. These politicians would rather see their rivals fail than our country succeed. It is all about power and many of our political leaders will do or say anything to gain that power. They don't dare cross party lines and disagree with their party, lest they be considered disloyal mavericks. Our community leaders have learned to do the same over the years. Can you imagine a successful corporation, sales department or functional family performing in this kind of atmosphere? It would be a sure remedy for disaster.

Weak leaders do not focus on uniting, they just focus on dividing. There is an old saying. "When the elephants fight, the ants take a hell of a beating." We, as citizens, are ants and are taking a hell of a beating from this kind of leadership.

When corporations do not grow, the head of the corporation is replaced. When communities do not grow, the leaders blame everyone outside the community. They never blame themselves or the individuals within their own community. For a business to function and grow it must have strong leadership and a logical, well thought-out strategy that each member of the company is responsible for executing. There must be communication among departments, with everyone working together for a common goal. Good performance is applauded and poor performance recognized and improved. In other words, before they look at outside forces preventing them from succeeding, they need to

> "When bad behavior is defended, it is encouraged."
> -- Chuck Togias

get their house in order. Abe Lincoln said, "A house divided against itself cannot stand." When corporations are divided, they're vulnerable to competitive attacks. The same holds true for our country, which is divided and very vulnerable.

Communities need strong leadership working together for the common good of its citizens. Communities that continue to have a lot of gangs and unrest are a result of weak community leadership.

Justice System: Lost Focus

The justice system has completely lost its focus. It no longer encourages truth; it has simply become a procedural system. Bold statements? Sure. But, to quote our courtroom friends, "Consider the facts." The judicial system is not looking for the truth – it's enforcing proper procedures. So while you and I may say that finding a dead body in a trunk is pretty damning, the System, with help from loop-hole savvy lawyers, would say, "Yeah, but it wasn't obtained properly, so it's inadmissible." Never mind that it's evidence of the crime. What's missing here is the truth. When the truth is absent, God forbid what fills its void.

It's even gotten to the point where the very well-off clients – and their equally financed lawyers – hire jury consultants to ascertain which jurors would be favorable to their case. In other words, they try to stack the deck. In search for the truth? I think you know better. Look at one of the more famous trials of the past century. I think I could have gotten O.J. Simpson off after the jury was selected.

So, Chuck, what does all of this have to do with sales? Well, a customer-focused sales rep will do the exact opposite of the Judicial System. In their client needs analysis, they are trying to find out the truth – every recommendation has to be based on facts. That is why customer-focused sales people are so admired by not only their clients, but also the entire industry.

On television I watch as these lawyers or law professors try to legitimize and defend the system. They try to pass it off as moral and ethical, even when they know justice did not prevail. It offends me. If they would only describe the system honestly – accurately relate what it has become – I would not be as offended. It is a procedural system. That is its focus.

Do not try to hide your identity, it only makes things worse. Change who you are and become more customer-focused or have the courage to tell it like it is.

Truth is not really truth. What is obvious is not obvious and what is a crime may not really be a crime. Preventing the truth from even entering the courtroom is a useful tactic for a trial attorney. Juries have to make a decision without many of the facts.

No wonder they are wrong so many times – they're shooting a target in the dark. This frustrates me so much because I hate things being complicated. I like things to be clear and simple, based on the truth always.

The Judicial System's two biggest compromises:

1. The system is no longer logical to anyone outside it. Judges and defense attorneys will defend their actions as within the law no matter how bizarre the outcome seems.

2. The system is no longer focused on finding the truth. It is much more interested on following procedures.

When logic and truth are missing from your organization, beware the end is near. Yet the judicial system has been able to flourish and in my opinion, here is why:

1. No competition – we only have one judicial system.

2. No accountability – many of our politicians are lawyers and they feed the system for their benefit.

It is only natural for them to do so. If most of our politicians were cab drivers we would all be required to take a cab to work. We have 5% of the world's population and 70% of the world's lawyers. There's gotta be a joke in there somewhere.

I mean, come on, what does 'inadmissible evidence' mean? Does it mean the evidence is not truthful or does it mean the process was not followed to obtain the evidence?

I once asked a lawyer who was running for judge to give me

his opinion on a hypothetical situation. "Suppose you saw a videotape of a murder being committed," I began. "There's no doubt about who killed the victim. But the videotape was obtained without following proper procedure and was inadmissible. There was no other evidence to link the criminal to the crime and he walked a free man. Is that justice," I asked him. He said that it was 100% correct to free the killer because the procedure was not followed. This type of logic is only logical to the judicial system.

I give the judicial system as an example of how losing focus can damage integrity. I want my readers to be aware of this so they will examine their business and personal practices closely.

For the record, I showed a New York State Supreme Court judge a draft of this book and he took exception to this section. He wanted to know what made me an authority of the judicial system.

I explained to him that I'm not an authority of the judicial system and its procedures, but I am an authority on truth and logic. And I can tell — just as any other semi-intelligent observer can — that the judicial system and its procedures are no longer focused on truth or logic.

If your business practices are based on truth and logic, your marketing focus can be clearly defined. Your customers will know what to expect when doing business with you. Truth should be the cornerstone of your business. Never compromise the truth or justify deceitful practices. Your company has competitors; and customers can, and will, go elsewhere.

Political System: Lost Integrity

This same mentality is used in our political system. Accuse your opponent first without revealing all the details, hide, and defend anything that can be used against you.

The system is complicated. The passage of laws is complicated. Many times legislation that is passed actually has nothing to do with the original intent of that legislation. It is most unfortunate that both systems have come to this.

Let us look at an example of something fair to everybody that lawmakers would never pass. The Flat Tax is a tax with a fixed rate for all goods and products bought. The more you buy the more you are taxed. The wealthy would obviously buy more, so they would be taxed more. It sounds fair right? The problem is, it is not complicated. In other words, it is too simple – we could all figure out our taxes very easily. That is not a good thing for a lawyer lobbyist to hear. Simple is a very bad word with lawyers. Where the Judicial System shows us the dangers of lost focus, the

other. And I am much more afraid of those who are not in power than those who are, because those not in power will do anything to undermine those who are. It becomes so subversive that we no longer have to worry about the enemy outside – the enemy inside is killing us.

The 2004 election was a lay-up for the democrats if they only attacked the issues, not the opponent. When you ask a Democratic Party loyalist why they did this – why they focused on personal attacks instead of the issues – they say because they attacked us first. Can't you just hear their collective mothers: "If so and so jumped off a bridge, would you follow?"

Studying success is very important to avoid pitfalls. Ronald Reagan left the White House with a 62% favorable rating. They said at his funeral that he never made an adversary an enemy. That is a great model for both parties to follow.

In business, never attack a competitor personally and never lose your integrity. It is the beginning of the end. Do the opposite of most politicians and you should be highly respected in your industry.

Media vs. Judicial

A war always rages between the media and the judicial system.

Especially during high profile trials. I, for one, think that in this situation the media is given a real bad rap. In my opinion, lawyers are always vilifying the media to take attention away from their behavior. It is ironic for a lawyer to accuse the media of not telling the truth. Have you ever heard a trial attorney say his client was guilty of anything...ever?

The media has a real difficult job. They are trying to uncover the truth without being able to secure all the facts. Who do you think tries to keep the truthful incriminating facts from being heard? It is certainly not the media. The media many times are like jurors, to come to any conclusion they have to almost guess.

When lawyers prevent the truth from being heard by the jury they say it is proper procedure. When the media, without all the facts, is wrong with their conclusions, the lawyers say it is a willful distortion of the truth. Give the media all the facts and I am sure their accuracy in reporting will be greatly enhanced. Let us start holding lawyers, judges and the judicial system as accountable as they hold the media. The lawyers for any and every missed statement hold the media accountable. What if we held the judges and lawyers to the same standard? Let us start to track criminals who have been set free by the judicial system through a technicality in procedure. Was society made safer? How many thousands of citizens have been violated as a result of a court case being dismissed based on some minor technicality? I am sure the numbers would be staggering. I am also sure the judicial system would defend their actions and never suggest changing the system.

I, for one, think that most media professionals are dedicated to doing the best and most credible job they can. I also feel that in these high profile trials the judicial system is the media's biggest problem, not the other way around. None of my conclusions pertains to those in the media that go out of their way to distort the truth. Although they are in the minority, they do exist and damage the only thing they have to sell, their credibility.

I do not have a negative view of all attorneys. I feel some prosecutors and corporate attorneys are more credible than attorneys who defend violent criminals because they can stick to the facts. Really, I am condemning the system more than the attorneys that have now inherited the system. The system has become very complicated and out of the attorney's control, so they work within it. I just wish they would not justify the system when injustices occur.

Success or Failure Should Be Determined By Results. Not Procedures.

When my sales department planned advertising campaigns for a client, we determined our success or failure on the results of the campaign. If the client's business did not improve, we would take the full responsibility for the failure, not justify it. When you admit you are wrong, a couple of things happen and they are both positive. First, when you admit a mistake and correct it, you will improve. Second, you will keep your credibility with your staff and clients.

If ever your company is engaging in practices that do not benefit clients or employees, change those practices. Do not defend them. You are jeopardizing your business, as well as your credibility. Be truthful with yourself and others and you will be held in high regard.

Misguided Recognition

As much as we may think otherwise, we live in a society of idol worshippers. How else can you explain our infatuation with, and worship of, high profile people such as entertainers and athletes. Even when some of these so-called icons have weak morals and values, they are admired. Role models determine some people's outlook in life. When their role models are in trouble, they are sad. If those role models are threatened, fans will risk their personal identity to defend them. That's quite scary.

A great example of this is Michael Jackson's fan base. Now I have no idea if he is a pedophile. I do know that a forty-eight year-old man who admits to sleeping in the same bed with children who are not his own is not normal in our society. Indeed, most would consider it very peculiar. Yet at his trial, Michael Jackson's obsessed fans surrounded the courthouse. They were screaming, crying and doing anything they could do to influence the media, jurors and the nation of his innocence, regardless of the truth. If there were a video that revealed his guilt, they would not have cared. The only thing his fans knew was that Michael Jackson was being attacked, and they were there to defend him. All I could think of was the Jim Jones followers who all committed suicide because of their blind loyalty to a madman. How many of those obsessed supporters would have been there if he were not a pop star? Can you imagine what those same people might do if someone, not famous, living in their neighborhood exhibited the same peculiar tendencies? Recognizing someone for a job well done is very important. Idolizing someone is rather pathetic.

If people with weak values are who you look up to, you have

already compromised your values. Admiring role models with questionable character will eventually affect your behavior and attitude. Teenagers who worship entertainers who endorse violence and criminal behavior will eventually participate in that behavior. Adults who worship political figures who lie and cheat are actually condoning that behavior and setting an awful example for their children. Loyal Republicans and Democrats do this everyday and jeopardize their own integrity when they continue to support members of their party who have lied and cheated. They justify their loyalty by trying to minimize the criminal act, unless, of course, it's the opposition that has been caught. Then they go for the jugular.

It takes courage to stand alone for truth. That's why I have always admired Senator Joseph Lieberman (D-CT). For the record, I am not a Democrat. But I respect Senator Lieberman because he always stands on principle, even when it threatens to erode his base of supporters. He did so by condemning former president Bill Clinton in the Monica Lewinsky situation. He also did so standing by President George W. Bush, for the most part, regarding the war in Iraq. I respect any politician, of any party, who stands not only for what his party tells him, but also for what his conscience tells him.

But it's not just the (few) principled people in power who we should respect. We should recognize and respect those who take pride in what they do; those who do their jobs with honor and integrity. Regardless of the job. Auto mechanics, house painters, computer analyst, teachers, nurses and firefighters – all are very important occupations in our society, all take talent and all deserve our respect.

My wife and I were in New Orleans for a training conference. For breakfast one morning, we went to Harrah's Casino where we enjoyed a terrific breakfast. Our short-order cook, Ernel Rufuge Sr., cooked our omelets to perfection and his attention to detail made breakfast a pleasant experience. I mention Ernel because he takes more pride in his job than many people in much higher-profile positions. And because of that, Ernel deserves a level of respect that most in our superficial society would deny him.

Start recognizing ordinary, hard-working people for their accomplishments. They are usually very deserving and will appreciate it.

Whatever your occupation, do the best you can to achieve success. Be knowledgeable in your industry. Have a dedicated work ethic and seek a lot of input from your peers to achieve higher levels. Most important, focus on your talents and not on worshipping others. You can only give 100% attention to one thing. It might as well be your personal growth rather than to stroke someone's over inflated ego.

As far as society is concerned, I recommend that you never idolize anyone. I look up to God – never my fellow man. If you are going to have a role model, make sure that their values are as important as their talents. Great morals and ethics should be how role models earn respect from their fans. Remember – focus on improving your talents, not someone else's fame.

> "If a man is called to be a streetsweeper, he should sweep streets even as Michelangelo painted, or Beethoven composed music, or Shakespeare wrote poetry. He should sweep streets so well that all the hosts of heaven and earth will pause to say, here lived a great streetsweeper who did his job well."
>
> --Martin Luther King, Jr.

CHAPTER TWO

Corporate Culture:
LEADERSHIP BEGINS AT THE TOP

So we've seen what the lack of leadership in our country has done to some of our most hallowed institutions. Now, it's time to fight back with good old-fashioned leadership skills. The first of which is being customer-focused. In this chapter, we will be reviewing the elements that are needed in developing a customer-focused culture.

Whether you're in a large corporation or a small business, you can take these elements and formulate a strongly worded customer-focused statement. You would gather management first to create a customer-focused philosophy and then develop a Mission Statement, set of values and a competitive edge. These would serve as the vocal point for your culture. You would then gather each department to formulate added values as well as standards and disciplines specific to each department in support of the new culture.

Being customer-focused means focusing on people. Life is about building strong relationships with family, friends and business associates. If the customer-focused culture is to be successful, everyone must understand that everything revolves around the customer. Delighting each customer is everyone's job responsibility. Always.

A very important element of the culture is employee empowerment. Empowerment is earned – each employee should be immersed in the process before given empowerment. Their attitude must be beyond question, and they should be monitored weekly to ensure implementation of the system. Once employees have earned their empowerment, they must be responsible for its execution. A company is only as good as its weakest employee. Each employee must be an added value problem-solver with clients, peers and vendors.

Mission Statement

Your Corporate Mission Statement is a clarity of purpose that the entire company must embrace. It is a rallying cry that unites all employees and departments for a single purpose. It is the number one job priority throughout the company and must be clearly defined. A successful mission statement must revolve around delighting the customers. All employees from the CEO down must understand its importance. Your mission statement gives your corporation an identity.

Customers as defined in a customer-focused culture include clients, peers and vendors. Employees are very important; a company must have unity within before it can be focused on the clients and vendors. The culture is developed from the inside out. As Abe Lincoln said when the South wanted to secede from the Union, "A house divided against itself cannot stand."

> "A house divided against itself cannot stand."
> --Abraham Lincoln

When I work with companies to help them formulate a corporate mission statement, we focus on delighting our customers not satisfying them. We try to make the statement go beyond the normal company mentality. I always include the word *ENTHUSIASTIC* in every mission statement I help formulate. That is one of my five favorite words because it makes the statement special in the minds of the employees. When you are enthusiastically helping your customers, you will have a successful outcome.

Focus on delighting your customers, not simply satisfying them.

After the Mission Statement is completed, following the rest of the lessons in this book will ensure that the company culture will change. The statement is a driving force for implementation. Management has a key role in developing the statement and the implementation of the system.

By the way, in case you were wondering, my five favorite words are: accountable, consistent, disciplined, enthusiastic and teachable. Each of these words is important for success, and I'll detail them a bit more later.

Philosophy

Companies formulate their identity when they create a focus. A company's focus can be based on one of three possible things: price, product or people.

When a company focuses on price, they are very vulnerable internally and externally to competitive attack. The employees know that the company's main interest is in price and profit. The message they receive is that profit and prices are king. They (the people) are secondary in this process and know they are dispensable and there is very little loyalty.

When a company focuses on product, they are also very vulnerable. First, products can be easily compared with price. And second, very few products are truly that much better than the competition. Essentially, they're all the same. So if the products are the same and the price is easy to overcome, you have only one thing to really focus on: people.

Funny, when you ask most companies if they are customer-focused they will emphatically reply "Yes." They feel that they satisfy their customers every day and only customers that are impossible to please are the exception.

However, their perspective of customer satisfaction is only measured from their company's point of view. They assume if they are courteous, and sell their product at a reasonable price, they have made the customer happy.

But a true customer-focused philosophy results in a culture with the following indicators:

1. Employees are happy and morale is upbeat.
2. Employees are promoted on their ability to create happy and delighted customers.
3. Departments communicate well and work seamlessly and effectively.

4. Managers define expectations and monitor results in a caring, disciplined environment.

5. Products and services reflect the company's desire to super-serve the customer.

6. Sales reps listen first to determine the customer's need before selling anything.

7. Sales reps understand that the most important thing they sell is ideas.

8. Sales reps are always solving problems after the sale for their customers.

9. Customer-Relations Departments are non-existent. If everyone is doing their job, a Customer-Relations Dept. is not needed.

10. The head of the company is always available for the employees and customers.

The result of a customer-focused philosophy is loyal customers. And loyal customers are the key to increasing revenues and market share.

The great thing is, this is really not a complex formula. Really, if you consistently deliver on the following three things, you will develop deeper loyalty among your customers:

1. Quality products that are dependable to the consumer.

2. Enthusiastic employee attitudes toward the customer.

3. Fair pricing.

Loyal customers will help companies increase revenues and market share. Customers who feel that you have always provided them with the help they need when making a purchase will think of you first when referring and making another purchase. They will look to you as a problem solver with results that are not only helpful, but also will save or make them money in the long run. You will become the most important part of the sales equation.

When an entire company – from the CEO to the hourly employees – are trained in this process the customers benefit. The important factor is to show the customer that they are very important. The CEO is key to the success, as he or she must set the standard by providing the authority and the example. The person who sweeps the floor must do his or her part to provide a clean and neat environment for the customer and the employees. Everyone is important; each is a key factor in the equation.

When the customer benefits, the business grows. Period. We are all in the game of positioning. Positioning ourselves as an added-value resource that individuals and organizations will find very difficult to live without. Providing your knowledge, expertise and problem solving abilities to your customer will give you that added-value, competitive advantage.

Core Values

Just as functional families follow a set of family values, a successful company must likewise define and monitor a set of core values for itself. The core values will provide guidance, clarity and integrity for all employees to follow. Once set, these rules *must not be compromised.* Period. No gray area. They must be defined to all employees, new and current. All employees must know that if they do not embrace your core values, they will not work for your company.

The problem is our society has become so politically correct that many people have adopted a universal value system. Nothing is out of bounds; everything and everyone, no matter what their behavior, should be accepted. Values based on your religious or environmental upbringing are considered out-dated and politically incorrect. It's even gotten to the point where many of us are afraid to disagree with things that we feel are morally and ethically wrong.

That's dangerous. As the old saying goes, "If you don't stand for something, you stand for nothing."

> "If you don't stand
> for something,
> you stand for nothing."

There is nothing wrong — and everything right — with formulating a strong, uncompromising value system. A value system that is determined by your morals, ethics and attitude. If you have strong morals and ethics and a great attitude, you will have strong values. When your personal values are strong, it's a good idea to only seek friends and companies that share these values. You will be very uncomfortable around people with weak values. People, as well as institutions, who embrace weak values are always compromising themselves.

Too many businesses give in to hiring the wrong people for the job, promoting based on longevity, and even lowering their standards to satisfy the loudest, least effective employees for fear of lawsuits.

When I do background checks on potential employees, I never call a reference. In sales, I call their customers to find out how they, the customer, see the sales rep. If any mention of bad attitude ever surfaces, the interview is over. Great customer-focused companies always hire employees with strong character. You can train employees in proper job techniques. It is much more difficult to improve someone's weak values.

Customer-focused companies must have a disciplined, defined value system to be able to consistently and effectively serve their customers. I can't emphasize enough: a company's core values should never be compromised.

When you are adopting a strong set of values, get the input of the management team and key employees. And make sure your values include the following:

1. Development – Every customer-focused company should be dedicated to improving employee effectiveness and efficiency through training, with a strong emphasis on uncompromising values.

2. Product – Your company should always strive to have the best product, performance and value.

3. Customer – Every employee's job is to super serve the customers internally and externally.

Strong, uncompromising ethical and moral values make employees proud to work for the company. They also make customers proud to do business with the company.

True Competitive Edge: Why should I do business with you?

Whenever you are trying to secure business there is one question that you must answer whether it is actually stated or not. The question has two parts and is as follows:

1. Why should I do business with your company?
2. Why should I do business with you? In other words, how do I benefit when I do business with you or your company?

You must answer that question in every sale unless you are always the lowest priced. Your mission statement gives your corporation an identity. Your competitive edge should give you an identity.

Sales people typically do something that makes no sense to me – they take themselves out of the sales equation and hide behind

> Your mission statement gives your corporation an identity.
> Your competitive edge should give you an identity.

product and price. The problem is when they do so, the customer can make an easy comparison. Product and price are very easy to compare. All the other things that go with the sale are harder to compare. Problem solving ideas, exceptional service, industry knowledge, and the perfect recommendation are impossible to compare.

"If it is to be, it is up to me."

The sales rep who understands that they are the key to a successful sale is invaluable. Let me give you an illustration. Say you're new in an area and want to buy a house. Wouldn't you go to a real estate agent who has knowledge of the area? You'd give them your specifications and they would use their knowledge to find you the perfect home. Their recommendation would be invaluable to you.

Some years ago, I was doing a sales presentation for a real estate company and was shocked by what I heard. Sales reps told me that their job was to show many houses and let the buyer make the choice. I told them that after they conduct the Client Needs Analysis, it was their job to find three houses and recommend one. They disagreed and told me that their job was to show houses because the buyer knows more about what they want than the sales person does. One woman was very adamant and insisted I was wrong. So I asked her how many houses she had sold that year. She said 44. I asked her how many houses

> Your competitive edge is not your product or your price. It's you.

the average buyer purchases in a year. She said one. "So you sell 44 homes, they buy one, and they know more about houses than you do?" I asked.

The room was silent.

The most important thing you must understand as a sales person is that you are the key to the sale. You must immerse yourself in the process. When you give well thought-out recommendations focused on fulfilling every need and improving your customer's situation, you are a tremendous resource.

Your competitive edge is not your product or your price. It's you. Your ability to understand the need and solve the problem will help you build long-term relationships. There is only one objection that you have to overcome and that's "I see no value in you or your product for me." That is why you should feature your ability and worth first, then your product.

Added Values
"Added values make you unique and your company credible."

Developing your company's added values is much tougher than it sounds. Adhering to them, tougher still. Start by creating a list of defined services that you will provide your customers – well beyond the normal "product at a price." The benefit that you provide will position you and your company as a valuable resource in the customer's mind.

Employees of each department should list the special services and products they provide to super-serve the customers. Everyone's attitude is focused on pleasing the customer.

What you are really doing is positioning you and your company differently than the other companies in the industry. Added values make you unique, and your company credible. They also help you position your competitor as less than cooperative without ever saying a bad word.

Think of all the things you can do that are important to your customer and are not industry standards. Create a list (define expectations) then monitor the list for execution. The key is not the list, but making sure you provide the services on the list continually.

Recently I was training a utility company's sales department. During my client needs analysis I found out they were the highest priced supplier of gas and electric products in their industry. Their competitors sold products at a lower price and positioned them as too expensive. So I asked a simple question: How does it benefit my company to do business with you? I divided them into three groups to contemplate the question. The next two hours were very difficult for them, but they formulated a list of important added values that helped to overcome the price objections they faced. It gave their company an identity they did not have previously.

The following are some of the added values we created to give the company a corporate identity with their customers. These added values were separated into two categories, Business and Relationships. Here are a few:

BUSINESS	RELATIONSHIPS
Assist customers in energy budget preparation.	Plan social outings (golf, sporting events)
Provide customized savings analysis	Send Christmas gifts
Provide customer friendly contracts	Send customized welcome letter
Always be available (pagers, cell phones, secretary, Vmail, Email)	Provide complimentary passes to industry seminars
Be a customer advocate (listen to customers and solve problems)	Client lunches
Act as an energy consultant for non-commodity issues.	Make contributions to client's favorite charity.

These are some of the added values that the utility company now provides their customers.

Your defined added values give you and your company an identity. Your identity is important if you are being attacked for being high priced. You must have a reason as to why you are higher priced and a better value.

In order to stay ahead of competitors, you must execute your values continually. As years go by your added values will become industry standards. This will allow you to become leaders of your industry with your customers and competitors. Try this session with your company. It will prove to be fun and thought provoking.

Standards and Disciplines

"It is impossible to be customer-focused without defined and monitored standards and disciplines."

To insure the execution of a customer-focused environment, you must define your standards and disciplines. Know that it is much easier to formulate a customer-focused philosophy than it is to execute it.

The process begins by management defining their own standards and disciplines; they must serve as the role model for the entire company and continually demonstrate commitment to the new culture.

After management has been trained, each department must develop their own Standards and Disciplines. These will be specific to each department and must be monitored continually to ensure execution. Great companies do what they say and say what they do. Defined standards and disciplines that are monitored *guarantee results*.

Here are a couple of examples of good defined standards and disciplines:

> Great companies do what they say and say what they do.

1. Phone calls – All morning phone calls are to be returned before lunch, all afternoon calls are to be returned before leaving for the day. *No exceptions.*

2. Meetings – Arrive five minutes early, with written agenda, pen and pad. Create a dated action plan for follow-up after every meeting.

3. Punctuality – Always be on time. Period. It's not only courteous, it's professional. It shows that you are serious about doing business and that you care.

I'll give you a real example – a humbling one at that – of why having good standards and disciplines are so important.

When I was selling radio advertising many years ago I was not always punctual. Our station never defined standards and disciplines. In fact, we never discussed the importance of being on time. So when I walked into a client's office ten minutes late for an appointment, I thought nothing of it. I introduced myself and started to explain the benefits of our radio station. The client stopped me short: "How dare you be late for our scheduled meeting. Who do you think you are?"

I tried to apologize but he threw me out of his office.

I had no defined expectation or monitored results. In other words, our station had weak leadership.

At first, I was angry, and then I was embarrassed. That evening, after reflecting on the situation, I realized I was 100%

wrong. My client was serious about doing business and that is why he fit me into his schedule. Yet I positioned myself very negatively in his mind. Not only was I unprofessional, I was also very rude. I made a pledge then and there that I would never be late for a client meeting again.

When I became the Sales Manager of the radio station, my staff and I created a list of standards and disciplines. At the top of the list was punctuality for all meetings in and out of the office. Everyone had to adhere to these standards or face the consequences. I would reprimand my employees rather than have them face the embarrassment that I had faced. It is impossible to be customer-focused without defined and monitored standards and disciplines. Your mission statement will have no meaning.

When developing these standards and disciplines, some will be for all departments and others will be specific for certain departments with special needs. All will be developed by the employees of those departments. When the employees have a say in the development of standards and disciplines, they will take ownership. When they take ownership, they are more apt to execute.

To insure enthusiastic customers and a top performing sales staff, management should implement a monitoring system.

In the field: create a list designed to ascertain customer input regarding service provided by your sales rep and company. This information will help your company continually upgrade their performance.

In the office: conduct one-on-one meetings with sales staff to monitor individual performance. Account list strategy, customer growth and service performance would be discussed in these meetings. The in-field visits and one-on-one meetings will help management monitor and improve on outstanding performance.

CHAPTER THREE

Management

IF PEOPLE AREN'T DEVELOPING UNDER YOU, ARE YOU A GOOD LEADER?

In this section, we will discuss the traits that will make you a good manager (also read 'good leader').

By the way, if people aren't developing under you, you are not a good leader. To be an effective manager, you must be a good developer of people so that every employee grows and becomes more effective under you. You must earn the respect of your staff. You must do what you say and say what you do. You must be morally and ethically sound and facilitate the development of strong standards and disciplines for each employee to follow. You should never lie to an employee or customer. You must celebrate success and discipline poor performance. Both are critical to employee morale and development. Finally, you must be a strategic thinker who has a vision for department and employee growth.

Remember, in a customer-focused environment, nothing matters but results. You can only achieve results when every employee has been developed and has a clear vision on good performance. Internal strife should never be tolerated. I always told my employees that everything is negotiable – their salary, vacation time – everything. Except attitude. You must have a great attitude when working with customers and employees alike, or work somewhere else. It is impossible to achieve aggressive goals when employees in your department are in conflict.

The team concept is a critical part of the success equation. Strong leaders have strong departments that share ideas and solve problems together.

And remember – leaders are collaborative, not dictatorial. Leaders define expectations and monitor results in a caring, disciplined environ-

> Leaders are collaborative, not dictatorial.
> They don't waiver on their principles.

ment. As you read this section, don't just think about how you can apply these elements at work. These same values can help strengthen your home and family as well.

Leadership

"The skillful general conducts his Army as if he were leading a single man by the hand."

Great managers are great leaders. Great leaders define expectations and monitor results. Giving a clear direction helps each employee know what is expected of him or her. When you monitor results, employees can be assured that consistent performance is expected.

Many managers will define expectations, but few of them monitor results. Look at job descriptions, for example. When most companies hire an employee, they review the job description. It defines each of the employee's job responsibilities. After the job description is reviewed, most companies or managers never refer back to it. In fact, most employees would not be able to define their job duties as defined in the job description.

Managers gain great credibility when they monitor performance. It allows them to encourage employees' strengths and help them overcome their weaknesses. Leaders are first and foremost developers.

Let me give you a great example. When I was training a broadcast company in Australia, I asked if they knew what Vince Lombardi was famous for. They overwhelmingly said football. I thought *Wow, even in Australia Vince Lombardi was famous.* The truth is, anyone who knows anything about American sports

> Vince Lombardi is famous for football, yet he never scored a point. That's a great leader.

thinks Vince Lombardi is synonymous with football. In fact, the most treasured trophy in all of football – the trophy given to the Super Bowl champion – is called the Lombardi Trophy.

Incredible, because Vince Lombardi never scored a single point. What he did do is show others how to score through his coaching and leadership. He will forever be remembered for it. Moral: In order to be a great leader, you must be a great developer of people.

How to spot a good leader. And a bad one.

All great leaders do the following:

1. Define expectations and monitor results.
2. Lead by example.
3. Develop their people.
4. Motivate by celebrating success.
5. Discipline non-performance.
6. Plan strategically.
7. Encourage employee input.
8. Unite, not divide.
9. Think logically.
10. Demand accountability.

Challenge: Next time you evaluate a leader, check off the items from this list that they do. Do they divide? Do they blame? Are they a good leader?

Encouraging employee input gives the employee ownership and helps in their development. Many years ago I used to formulate projections for each sales rep. It was an arduous process. I would review all their accounts and look for growth areas. I would also find new categories that could also help in their growth. In other words I gave them projections that were really mine. Then I got smart and turned the process around. I let them review growth areas with current and potential accounts. They formulated their own projections and two things happened:

1.) Since they formulated the projection and owned them, they were more successful at reaching and exceeding them;

2.) The projections they gave me were actually higher percentage-wise than the ones I used to give them. They were on commission and wanted to make as much money as possible.

To help them manage the process I would require a detailed action plan on how they would achieve their goals.

When developing your staff you must empower them to take ownership and make decisions. Great leaders are great developers. Great leaders get results leading by example, disciplining non-performance, uniting and demanding accountability. Leaders are interested in improving the lives of those around them and not afraid to admit mistakes.

Remember: Leaders earn the right to be leaders by the results they achieve, not by how loud they talk.

The 15 Steps to Successful Leadership

_____

① Always conduct your business beyond reproach.
Never lie - to employees or clients. Always act as a role model - do what you say and say what you do.

② Always evaluate employees on a consistent basis.
Recognize and encourage success so your employees will want to repeat their performance. Also, help identify and manage weaknesses so your employees can improve.

③ Never show employee favoritism.
Every employee should abide by department policies and standards.

④ Always respond in a timely manner to employee requests and problems.
Treat your employees' concerns as if they were your own.

⑤ Always formulate clear expectations with your employees.
Clearly define what you expect with every employee. Ask for employee input when defining job responsibilities.

⑥ Always keep lines of communication open.
Encourage your employees to discuss job-related subjects. Always make your time available for employee discussions.

⑦ Always stress employee involvement.
Encourage your employees to get involved and immersed in the day-to-day activities involving your department.

⑧ Always stress employee empowerment.
When employees are properly trained, give them the responsibility to make it happen.

(9)
Always encourage creative thinking.
Every employee should be encouraged to think as an added value,
creative problem solver.

(10)
Always make people development your number one job priority.
Remember, every person in your department is a reflection of your
ability to manage.

(11)
Always celebrate success through employee recognition.
Remember, "There is no success without celebration." Develop a
system that consistently recognizes good performers.

(12)
Always discipline non-performance.
When there is no discipline, the standard of excellence must decline.

(13)
Never say no without first saying,
"Let me try to find a way to help."
"No" should be eliminated from your new
customer-focused vocabulary as a first response.

(14)
Always be a strategist preparing your team to succeed.
Plans and strategies should always be formulated in the office,
not in the field. *The general who wins in battle makes many
calculations in his temple before the battle is fought.*" – Sun Tzu

(15)
Always make your employees and departments
accountable for their actions.

Strategic Thinking

"It is that in war, that the victorious strategist only seeks battle after the victory has been won." –Sun Tzu

For a leader to earn the right for leadership, he or she must have a clear vision for growth.

I am from an area in New York state where there has been little to no growth. Yet the citizens in that area still re-elect their political leaders repeatedly. We have a Senator in the area who has been re-elected for 25 years, even though in my opinion he has no vision on how to make the area grow.

In fact, he has been completely against a local developer who has a vision for constructing one of the largest malls/entertainment centers in the country. This politician has had many years to come up with his own vision for growth and never has, but he is adamantly against the developer's vision. I am not upset with the Senator because he is against the mall; I am upset that he has no vision for growth. I know what he is against – I just do not know what he is for.

Apparently, in politics you can get away with a lack of vision. In business, you cannot. If a manager cannot articulate his department's current status, what the vision for growth is and how he is going to achieve it, then he should be replaced and his power given to someone who can achieve this. If not, the competition will eat the company alive.

As I repeatedly state, in a customer-focused company, results are everything. If your customers, peers and vendors are benefiting, your company will grow. Leaders with strategic vision grow companies. As Sun Tzu says, "It is that in war that the victorious strategist only seeks battle after victory has been won." Strategists have vision and visionaries win.

There are three areas important for strategic planning by Management:

> **1. Job Descriptions** – Defining job responsibilities for each employee that prioritize, emphasize and monitor all job responsibilities. In addition, every job description should be used as a quarterly evaluation form.

> **2. Departmental Plans** – Management should complete these prior to the upcoming year to serve as a compass. These plans should articulate current departmental status, vision for growth and, most important, how to achieve that vision.

> **3. Training Manual** – People development insures company growth. When the manual is completed, it will become a clear, concise guide to help each employee achieve the highest level of performance.

Team Concept

A company should formulate a team concept to increase support among individuals and departments. I practiced this whole-heartedly when I was the General Sales Manager at a radio station. Everyone in the Sales Department was committed to helping each other grow. We would meet weekly, review every sales call each member made, and give input to try to secure each sale. We would ask questions to determine if the salesperson knew important information regarding the client's product and needs. We were relentless in trying to find problem areas that we as a staff could overcome. The exercise was not only helpful to the sales person who was closing the sale, but also to each of us who were helping in the process. It was helping us identify objections that we could be facing with our accounts in the future.

We would also review every objection that we have faced or could face, and discuss our options for solving the objection. We did this weekly and the growth we experienced was nothing short of phenomenal. Using this concept was in my opinion the number one reason that our AM and FM stations took a 55% share of revenue in a 21-station market and ranked #1 *in the USA*.

When you have good salespeople in your department, they have a moral responsibility to help every other sales person grow.

It is not just the Sales Manager's job to do so. When salespeople are involved in the growth of the department, they become leaders and earn great respect. Others in the department want to emulate them and do so by being helpful to their peers. It has a domino effect.

Not only do the sales people grow individually, but because they helped each other in the process, they grew very close as a group. Many people thinking and working together are a very formidable force.

Many companies never encourage their top sales people to interact with the rest of the sales staff. I did the opposite. My department knew from the day they came what our customer-focused team philosophy was and what was expected of them. I never hired someone and wondered if they were going to succeed. I always tried to increase the odds of success by the team concept.

In my opinion, there are only two reasons why your employee can fail: 1. You hire the wrong person; or 2. training was not adequate. The team concept helps to eliminate the training question.

Working together as a team pays great dividends.

Quotes for Management Growth

Managers have a difficult job because they must discipline non-performance and yet always celebrate success. They must be visionaries and great people developers. Good managers are focused on their people, departments, company and clients. A good manager must be customer-focused. One way to become a good manager is to learn from good managers. Here are some meaningful quotes:

"An army of lions led by a lamb will be defeated by
an army of lambs led by a lion."
--West Point

"It is that in war that the victorious strategist only seeks
battle after victory has been won."
--Sun Tzu

"If you give someone a fish you feed them for a day.
If you teach them how to fish, you've fed them for a lifetime."
-- Chinese Proverb

"The general who wins in battle makes calculations in his
temple before the battle is fought."
--Sun Tzu

"Losing should always be unexpected."
--Willie Davis (Green Bay Packers)

"Regard your soldiers as your children and they will follow
you into the deepest valleys; look on them as your beloved
sons, and they will stand by you even unto death."
--Sun Tzu

"There is no success without celebration."
--*Don Clifton*

"The skillful general conducts his army as if he were leading a single man by the hand."
-*Sun Tzu*

"If however you are indulgent, but unable to make your authority felt; kind hearted, but unable to enforce your commands; and incapable, moreover, of quelling disorder, then your soldiers must be likened to spoiled children; they are useless for any practical purpose."
-*Sun Tzu*

"Whoever loves discipline loves knowledge, but he who hates correction is stupid."
--*Proverbs 12:1*

"Management is simple; you define expectations and monitor results in a caring, disciplined environment."
--*Chuck Togias*

"Most great leaders I've met are simple men. People like Sam Walton and General Schwarzkopf – they're far from stupid, but basically very simple. I include myself in that category. I hate complexity. I think the world is already complex enough as it is without me making it more so. The principles of management and leadership are simple. The hard part is doing them, living up to them, not making excuses for ourselves. You know all those complex management theories? They're just an excuse for not facing up to how hard it is to live by some very basic principles."
-*H. Ross Perot*

CHAPTER FOUR

—

Sales

THE SECRET TO CONTROLLING
THE SALE: SHUT UP

In this section, we will discuss one of the most important characteristics of a successful sales person: the ability to listen. When the sales rep is listening, they are in control of the sale. Information is the key, and the best way to gather information is to listen. Sun Tzu says, "The greatest weapon in warfare is spies." The sale is controlled with information.

I'm not talking about passive listening. I'm talking about active listening, where you are absorbing the information you hear in order to create a more effective actionable plan, designed around solving client needs. Once you define the client's needs, you are in a better position to present creative ideas and solve problems.

Then we'll discuss the next element needed to insure results for the client: Your product knowledge.

In our competitive section, I said the customer focused reps competitive edge is their expertise, empathy and problem solving ability. The expertise means you understand your product and your client's needs. When you do, ideas will flow. Creative ideas focus is to solve problems. When you solve problems, you have empathy and care about your client's success.

Sales is very simple when you use this formula. Listen and uncover needs, know your product and solve problems through creative ideas. When you do, you will build long-term relationships and become a valuable resource to your clients. Price will then become less of an issue.

The Selling Process: Information is the Key

In business, as well as in your personal life, gaining information is critical. The best way to gain information is to listen intently before speaking. It's not only courteous, it's also very important in building relationships. Strong relationships are everything if you're going to become successful. To me, success encompasses your business as well as the personal aspects of your life.

When you listen to someone and probe for more information, you are demonstrating that you care. You're illustrating the saying, "I don't care how much you know until I know how much you care." Whether you are trying to do business with someone or build a personal relationship, it is much easier if you are a good listener. The sales person who is listening is in charge of the sale. Not the one speaking.

> **Seek first to understand, then to be understood.**
> *-- Dr. Stephen Covey*

So you need to gain information. You have to find out the needs, problems and concerns of your client before you're ready to give your helpful suggestions. After you listen and probe for more information, you should take time to resolve the problem. In other words, take 50% of your time in your client needs analysis, 35% of your time solving your client's problems, 10% of your time in your presentation, and 5% in your close (see triangle on the next page). *It is not your job as a sales person to close; it is your job to solve the problem so the client will initiate the close.*

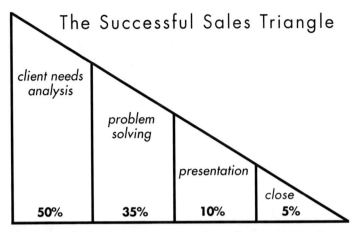

The Successful Sales Triangle

client needs
analysis

problem
solving

presentation

close

50%　35%　10%　5%

1. **Client Needs Analysis.** Listen intently to find out the need or problem.
2. **Problem Solving.** Always try to help your client improve their current situation. Sell ideas and always think out of the box.
3. **Presentation.** Clearly define your problem solving solutions. Give well thought out recommendations, not choices.
4. **The Close.** If you do the above well, the client will initiate the close.

When building a relationship, you must take time to listen first before making any recommendations. When you follow this procedure, you will become a valuable resource to your client. Great salespeople give great recommendations – not choices. Listening helps you come up with ideas, which is another valuable part of the sales relationship equation.

The selling philosophy is almost the opposite of what most car dealerships do. They spend 5% of their time in the client needs analysis, 10% problem solving, 35% in the presentation, and 50% of their time in the closing. When you spend 50% of your time closing a sale, you have no idea what the client really needs. And you probably don't care.

The *customer-focused sellers* spend 85% of their time ascertaining needs and solving problems. The *product sellers* spends 85% of their time in the presentation and close. The customer-focused seller is trying to help their clients. The product seller is trying to sell product and help him or herself.

What is even more damaging is the average automobile salesperson does not build long lasting relationships. They are always looking for new customers. Remember great sales people are great listeners, not fast talkers. When they do communicate, people will listen and benefit. In building long term relationships, become externally focused. In other words, find out about others rather than always talking about your product and self.

This is a good place for me to tell you about a longtime friend of mine, Peter Dourdas. Peter is the quintessential "rags-to-riches" example, and his story is important to this book because Pete ultimately earned his success by putting into practice a lesson that you'll find repeated over and over throughout these pages. Only, Peter didn't have the benefit of a book such as this; he had to learn his lessons the hard way.

Peter was raised in a low income, high crime neighborhood, the son of poor European immigrants who only spoke broken English. As a result of this environment, Peter grew into an angry, troubled young boy with very low self esteem. He had very few friends, no close relationships and was very unhappy. A kid on the path to self destruction if there ever was one.

So what happened? How did this angry young boy with a chip on his shoulder become such a successful businessman? What was the turning point?

"I just looked in the mirror one day and didn't like what I saw," he says.

Peter decided then and there that he was going to change. He was going to succeed. He was going to make something of himself. In order to do this, he knew that he first had to engage in some brutally honest self examination.

It was during his gut check that Peter realized he knew little to nothing about the few friends he did have. He was always too busy talking about himself and was never really interested in listening to what others had to say. *(Incidentally, this is the way most people sell.)*

Because Peter so desperately wanted friends, he intuitively decided to start listening more than he talked. You know where

71

I'm going with this now, don't you? The more Peter listened and became interested in what others had to say, the more they listened to him. The more information he gathered before reacting, the better off he was. The better he treat-

> You reap what you sow and sow what you reap.

ed others, the better they treated him. Before long, Peter began to develop strong friendships. And strong, healthy relationships are vital to success and happiness.

Today, Peter is the president of Dourdas Financial, Inc., a very successful financial planning business with offices in New York City and upstate New York. He's also on the Board of Directors for the YMCA, he's on the board of his church, and he has been a continual member of the prestigious Million Dollar Round Table (MDRT).

According to Peter, the number one reason for all of this success and happiness was his not-so-secret weapon:

"I became a good listener."

Listening gave Peter a new attitude on life. And ultimately steered him toward that which we all seek: a strong, loving family, a tight group of friends and a very successful career.

For a successful sales rep, listening and gaining information is the most important part of the sale. When you actively listen, two things happen that are vital in guaranteeing success:

1.) Information helps uncover needs and problems. This is important because without a need or problem there is no sale.

2.) Listening and empathizing with your customer helps build strong relationships.

Good relationships are a key element in sales as well as life. That is why I say again, it is the sales person who is actively listening to clients – not the one talking – who is in complete control of the sale. Sales is no different than life – to build solid relationships people have to know you care first. "I don't care how much you know until I know how much you care." Peter's clients and friends all know that he cares.

AVERAGE SALES PEOPLE VS. GREAT SALES PEOPLE
What it takes to be in the top 5%

Average Sales People *(95% of the sales population)*	**Great Sales People** *(5% of the sales population)*
1. Fast talkers	1. Great listeners
2. Presenting products is their priority	2. Understand the importance of gaining information
3. Spend 50% of the selling process closing the sale	3. Spend 50% of the selling process ascertaining needs
4. Sell product and price	4. Sell great ideas
5. Spend 35% of the selling process presenting their product	5. Spend 35% of the selling process problem solving
6. Continually sell their product	6. Continually available to solve problems
7. Give choices, not recommendations	7. Make specific recommendations
8. Focus on making commissions	8. Focus on client results
9. Not concerned with clients after the sale	9. Continues to build long-term relationships after the sale
10. Punctuality not a priority	10. Punctuality a priority

Great sales people create value and improve their customers' positions. The other guys just sell product.

TIPS TO IMPROVE YOUR SELLING PROCESS

CLIENT NEEDS ANALYSIS VS. BUDGET:

A good sales rep – a customer-focused sales rep – does not focus on a budget. A good sales rep focuses on creating ideas and solving client problems. Sales reps have no input in budgets created by their clients. Many of these budgets do not give the customer-focused seller enough money to truly solve the problem.

Let's say, for example, that a couple wants to purchase a home in an affluent area. They want 3,000 square feet, a fireplace, pool and highly accredited schools. The money they have allocated makes it impossible for the real estate agent to meet their needs. The agent's job is to either lower their expectations or find them the exact house they are looking for and to demonstrate how they can creatively pay for it. For instance, show how their budget is doable when the difference is spread over 30 years. Having their family in the right house – even though their budget was increased – will make the customer much happier in the long run. You will be creating a loyal customer.

RECOMMENDATION VS. CHOICE:

It's not your job as a salesperson to simply give your client a bunch of choices. It's your job to give a well-informed recommendation. The recommendation helps you stay in control of the sale and makes you valuable. If you take a lot of time to understand the client needs and know your product, you should always feel comfortable giving a specific recommendation. When you give a choice, you lose your most important asset – your problem solving expertise. Instead, you allow the client to solve the problem. This is not good in a customer-focused sales environment.

WRITTEN PRESENTATIONS:

Written presentations should always be very clear and simple. Each should have eight elements:

1. Title page
2. Table of contents
3. Objectives
4. Executive Summary
5. Need and Benefit
6. **Why? Why should anyone do business with you or your company?**
7. Fees
8. **References**

All of my proposals have #6, "Why do business with me?" and #8, "References." I consider these two sections the most important part of the proposal. In #6 you reiterate why you and your company are so valuable to the client. In #8 you give them a chance to call your references. Giving these references shows your client that you are confident in your company's past performances.

Also never bind a proposal. Each page should be discussed separately. If you give a bound proposal, the client will always go to the back for fees first. You must create value before discussing fees.

Selling Ideas
"If the idea is dynamic, price becomes less of an objection."

I've given a lot of seminars over the years. A whole lot. In each one, I ask sales professionals the same question:

"What do you sell?"

The vast majority say they sell a certain product or service. Then they go into details of their product benefits. Now don't get me wrong – product and product expertise is important. But it is not the most important thing you sell. The most important thing you sell is ideas. Ideas are *always* designed to help the customer. The same can't always be said of your product. If you are focused on improving the customer's business, and you have gathered lots of information, ideas will flow. Great ideas help the customer become more effective and efficient.

Many times your product or service is not fully utilized unless you have a unique idea on how to best implement it. That idea is a very important part of a truly successful sale. Only the true customer-focused reps can succeed with this method.

As I mentioned earlier, I was once the Sales Manager for a New York AM and FM radio station. When I first took over in 1978, we had a 17% share of revenue in a 21-radio station market.

By 1982 – just four short years later – we had a 40% share, and went on to have a 55% share, which was #1 in a medium to large market in the U.S. at that time. How did we do it? You guessed it - we were very customer-focused. The sales staff was led by a brilliant salesman named Arnie Rothschild.

When I hired Arnie, he inherited a list that billed approximately $100K a year. Within 3 years, he was billing close to $100K a month and had increased his salary (commission) *six times more* than his predecessor. Whoa! There was no great secret to Arnie's success. He simply had a great ability to sell ideas. The ideas Arnie came up with were always focused on his customer's growth. He would listen to find out the real need or problem, and then use all of his knowledge and resources to help his clients grow. As each client grew, so did Arnie. Until he became the #1 biller in our company's history.

Arnie still sells ideas, always focused on helping his client's grow. His current company, Normal Communications, sells transit advertising in Syracuse, Rochester and Buffalo. One of his sales reps sold 20 signs on the side of the bus to a cleaning company. During the run of the campaign, the advertising agency for the cleaning company called to cancel the advertising because the client said it was not working. They were not getting any phone inquiries and wanted the campaign to run out at the end of the month. Not to be deterred, Arnie told his sales rep to call the transit center and have them put every sign in upside down. The client's phone rang off the hook with potential customers calling to let the client know that their signs were upside down. The client thanked them for calling and signed many of them up for their services. Needless to say the client did not cancel their schedule. In fact, they renewed it.

To this day Arnie loves to create ideas to benefit his employees and customers. However, if you do not gain information, it is very hard to come up with creative ideas.

If the idea is dynamic, price becomes less of an objection. Sales is really simple. If you listen to customers with the sole purpose of helping them improve their situation, and if you sell ideas, each customer will benefit. As each customer benefits, you will start to build long-term relationships and develop a strong customer base. As your customer base grows, so will you.

You sell your goods and services everyday, and sometimes forget what you are paid to do. Especially if you are with a company that only focuses on increased sales and not on customer growth. To separate yourself from the average peddler, know that your greatest asset to your customer is your ability to formulate a creative idea designed to help their business improve. Arnie Rothschild did and still does, becoming very successful in the process.

Product Knowledge

Knowing your product is a fundamental rule of sales. If you are going to be successful in sales, you must first understand your product then your clients' needs. Then you must understand how your product can help them meet those needs. The more you know about both, the better equipped you are to get results. All customer-focused sales people have great product knowledge. When you do not know your product, your customer is not confident in you and your ability to solve the problem. In fact, weak product knowledge can directly affect any trust a customer will have in you and your company. Let me give you a simple example (yes, another one.)

My wife and I recently contracted to build a new home. We were assigned a designer whose job was to help us work with the builder's vendors to pick out flooring, appliances, cabinets, etc. The builder gave us an allowance for upgrades, so all we had to do was go to the showroom and pick out our items. Or so we thought.

The vendor who supplied the appliances and cabinets was

absolutely clueless. No product knowledge. He did not know the prices on the refrigerator, stove, dishwasher and washer/dryer. He could not give us prices on any of his products. Needless to say, that did not exactly instill confidence in my wife and me. We were very suspicious. Either he was pulling a con or he was just plain ignorant. For his sake, I hoped he was conning us. No one can be that ignorant.

The cabinet person was just as void of knowledge. She didn't have a kitchen cabinet design and didn't know what was considered an upgrade or any of the prices. Between the two of them, they knew little to nothing about their products or prices. We figured at this rate it would take us six months of traveling between Naples and Fort Myers to resolve the problem.

When we got home, we called the builder's sales rep as well as the designer to voice our displeasure. The sales rep was in disbelief. I immediately told him that we wanted to work with another vendor. After this experience, my wife and I felt very leery of the builder and the vendor. The vendor not only positioned himself negatively – but also did the same for the builder.

I wish the story ended here. I wish it was just a matter of poor product knowledge requiring a bit of customer service to correct. Unfortunately, we were so put off by our encounter that we dug a little further into the builder's company and discovered some highly questionable practices and sketchy integrity, which I won't go into here. We wouldn't have discovered it were it not for a few vendors with extremely poor product knowledge.

The real lesson here is that you *cannot* solve a customer's problems if you don't have product knowledge. It's impossible. You cannot complete the recommendation portion of your customer needs analysis without product knowledge. Information stimulates thought. The more knowledge you have of your product and the more knowledge you have of your client, the greater the ideas you can offer. In fact, gather as much information as possible and you will amaze yourself at the amount of ideas you can generate. I guarantee it.

Understand everything you can about your product, define your client's specific needs with a focus on solving the problem and your client will not be able to live without you.

Problem Solving

"You can insure the safety of your defense if you only hold positions that cannot be attacked." --Sun Tzu

When trying to position yourself as a valuable resource to your clients, your ability to solve problems is very important. Every business needs to surround themselves with problem solvers. These people do more than simply identify a need – they also have ideas on how to overcome that need.

I think it's this skill that makes doctors some of the most respected professionals. They have the ability to identify the need and solve the problem. When the doctor examines us, they are performing the customer-focused sales process as correctly and naturally as it can be done. Their job is to solve the problem. Period. They base their success on their ability to solve each patient's problem. They never try to disguise it. That is why the medical profession is so respected. (Also notice, they don't give you a bunch of choices for treatment – they give a recommendation.)

When you listen to your clients with the singular purpose of solving problems, you become a valuable resource. You become someone that the client cannot live without. Your problem-solving skills make it very difficult to be attacked by competitors. As Sun Tzu says, "You can insure the safety of your defense if you only hold positions that cannot be attacked."

Most companies, unfortunately, do not have a customer-focused, problem-solving culture. A couple of years ago my wife and I planned a trip to Washington, D.C., to see some friends. We made our reservations with USAir. The weather conditions leading up to our flight were questionable. In fact, a hurricane was approaching the East coast, heading for D.C. The day before we were scheduled to leave, the Washington Mass Transit closed for the first time ever.

Our friends called and suggested that we cancel our flight because everything was closed in Washington. So we called USAir and explained our situation. The representative told me that I had to reschedule and fly within seven days or pay a $100 cancellation fee. I explained to them that I would book the flight, but could not fly until three weeks later. I asked if they could please bend their policy, because of the hurricane. My rep (who obviously hadn't read this book) told me flat-out NO. Policy was policy. Thinking all I had to do was get to someone in charge, I went to the top of USAir to logically explain my problem. Apparently, USAir doesn't have a single employee with the authority to help the customer – even when it is logical to do so. And the company won't empower any of their employees to change the policy – regardless of the situation.

This type of corporate mindset is disastrous. Employees in great companies are empowered to insure happy customers. If you are a company that is going to prosper, you must think long term. Long-term thinking means you don't nickel and dime each customer. Employees are logical in their decision making and incorporate a philosophy that focuses on each customer. These companies build long-term relationships by allowing their employees to use good judgment when they deal with a customer. Companies with a customer-focused philosophy are fun to do business with. On the other hand, companies rigid in their policies are difficult to continue doing business with. I know my wife and I will never do business with USAir again, for any reason. We don't even check their fares anymore. In the short term, they made $200. In the long term, they will make zero from us.

Problem-solvers help you no matter what it means to their commission. Create a problem solving philosophy and encourage each employee to think out of the box.

The ability to solve problems is a slower process than selling a product at a price. It takes time to gather information; rarely can the sale be closed on the first visit. In fact, the goal of the first visit should be to gather information so you can start to stimulate thought for the next visit. Dedicated problem solvers have one purpose - to help their clients grow. They are very similar to dedicated doctors, whose sole purpose is to help their patients improve.

The auto industry is another example of the exact opposite approach: it's not about solving problems, it's about the product and the price. During the sale, the sales person very quickly gets to the presentation portion, which leads directly to the close. They are there to sell the product and have been trained to get to the close quickly. This process is not always in the customer's best interest and, because it is price focused, can be very easily attacked by another competitor. After the sale, their philosophy is again the opposite of a customer-focused environment. A perfect example is the manufacturer's warranty. On a 4-year/50,000 mile warranty, for example, the customer has to come back into the dealership for warranted service for 4 years/50,000 miles and never has to interact with the sales person. The manufacturer did their job for the dealership by warranting the automobile; but the dealership loses an opportunity. Most dealerships never have the salesperson interact with the customer after the contracts have been signed. In fact, management usually doesn't even want the sales person involved after the sale. They think it is a waste of time.

But the warrantee is a great opportunity for the sales person to build a great long-term relationship by being there to solve problems. Yet management discourages them from doing so. The car dealer is there to sell cars not to have their sales people build relationships. What a crazy system. The salesperson should be immersed in the sale and after the sale process. Whenever the customers come to the dealership for service, the salesperson should be notified and ready to listen and help. When the car is serviced, the salesperson should review the bill with his customer and have his customer notify him with any additional problems. Problem solvers love solving problems – not running from them. Problems solved make problem solvers look good and build long-term relationships.

Auto dealers get very upset because customers are so price sensitive. But what do they expect? They have created this problem with their before and after sales techniques. Their dealership is full of sales people, not problem solvers.

Remember – you become a valuable resource to your customer whenever you solve problems.

CHAPTER FIVE

Marketing
POSITIONING YOURSELF TO
BE A PROBLEM SOLVER

In this section, we will discuss marketing techniques. Knowing your target and what is important to them is critical. When you create a mass-marketing campaign, you have to identify the target. It's imperative to know the age, sex, income and lifestyle of the buyer most likely to purchase your goods or services. Then you have to identify their key buying considerations such as price, quality, prestige, etc. When you know who is most likely to buy your product and their key buying consideration, you can create a positioning statement. Your statement must be based on the key buying consideration of the target. For example, Wal-Mart has identified their target and their key buying considerations.

The key buying consideration for their shopper is price. Therefore, Wal-Mart's positioning statement is "Always low prices. Always." Wal-Mart wants to position their store in the target's mind with low prices.

Advertising campaigns are designed to affect the target's perception of the product. In other words, it is not what the product contains that is as important as what the target perceives about the product. Many times, there is very little difference in products; the difference is in the perception of the product in the target's mind. Positioning products is so important that companies spend hundreds of millions of dollars a year to do so. Positioning will determine their success or failure.

It is just as important to position yourself, as well as your company and product, in your client's mind. When you understand the importance of positioning yourself first as an added value problem solver, you will reap the rewards. It is easy to compare products and price – much harder to compare a dedicated problem solver.

Your clients benefit when they do business with you. As a result, they will want to continue to do business with you. When they think of your company or products, they will automatically think of a successful outcome because of your involvement. That is how to build long-term relationships.

Positioning yourself as the key element in the sale will only enhance your position in your target's mind. You will have complete control of the account – price will become less of a factor.

Positioning Techniques

Al Ries and Jack Trout wrote my favorite marketing books. They wrote the *22 Immutable Laws of Marketing*, *Positioning: the Battle for the Mind* and Al Ries wrote the book *Focus*. These books were written years ago, but I still highly recommend them – they are very informative, humorous and well-written.

In the *22 Immutable Laws of Marketing*, Law 15 is the law of candor. When you admit a negative, the prospect will give you a positive. Can you imagine how a politician could gain integrity by admitting a negative? We would believe anything they said after that. Someone who's truthful about their flaws are usually truthful about everything. I think people demonstrate their honesty when they volunteer negative information about themselves. Most politicians only volunteer negative information about their opponents and their opponent's party, which positions them negatively.

When you try to position your product or yourself in your

prospect's mind, you have to know your target, and what they are most interested in. In the book, *Positioning: the Battle for the Mind*, the author tells us that the mind works like a ladder. It prioritizes everything. The first three rungs are most important in the target's mind.

The key position on this ladder, of course, is the first rung. That's where you want your product or yourself. A customer-focused rep always positions their problem-solving skills first, and then their product. Products can be easily compared; problem-solving ability cannot.

The best thing about being positioned as a problem solver is that there is little need to change. Keep your focus on helping each client succeed and continue to do so forever. The corporate, management and sales elements are subject to little change when they are customer-focused. Therefore, your positioning techniques remain the same. The smoke and mirrors approach always changes; the customer-focused approach does not. One is designed for a quick sale. The other, for happy customers and long-term relationships.

Sun Tzu again: "You can insure the safety of your defense if you only hold positions that cannot be attacked." Problem-solving techniques insure the safety of your position.

Marketing Yourself

With every sales call you make, you are positioning yourself and your company. Sometimes positively, sometimes negatively. Your industry also positions you positively or negatively. Used car salesmen and criminal defense attorneys aren't usually thought of in the most positive light. That doesn't mean that all used car sales people or criminal defense attorneys are bad, it means that their industry has pre-positioned itself over the years in a negative light.

The phrase "selling yourself first is critical" is extra important for a customer-focused salesperson. A customer-focused salesperson must let their customer know quickly that solving problems is their only business. We used to have a sign hanging in our radio sales office that said, "We will never ask for your business unless we can help

> We will never ask for your business unless we can help improve it.

improve it." We, as a sales staff, would review our client's needs and determine whether we had the capabilities to help. If not, we would walk away from securing the business. It is very hard to walk away from business, but it is critical if you are to position yourself as an added value problem solver to your clients. Your staff should separate itself from the industry sellers. I never wanted anyone to say that our reps were typical industry sellers. That is a very negative remark.

When positioning yourself you have to remember three things.

1. Listen first. Let your clients know that you are there to listen to their needs and then help find solutions for those needs.

2. Create ideas. Once you identify the need, use your resources to come up with a creative idea.

3. Solve problems. Always try to find solutions for client's problems whether it concerns your product and service or not.

When your clients know that your one focus is helping them succeed, you will become a resource that they cannot live without.

This is an important step in building long-term relationships.

—

CHAPTER SIX

Personal Growth

As I stated in the beginning of this book, if you follow these lessons you'll become more than a better *sales*person. You'll become a better overall person. There are three very important areas in your growth that will help you accomplish this: Belief, Attitude and Self Esteem.

Belief

Belief is very important, as long as it's founded on strong moral and ethical principles. If it's not, it can be dangerous. It's for their beliefs that some fanatics in Arab countries tie explosives to themselves and blow themselves and others up, hoping to take out as many innocents as possible in the process. Strong belief?

Absolutely. Will it lead to personal growth? Not likely. Because while these fanatics have strong beliefs, they have misguided values. A strong belief system based on good values usually involves belief in God, family, company and self, with a great respect for others. Sound values with strong belief reaps rewards. When you know you are doing the right things, your belief increases.

Belief is not only necessary for personal growth. It's also one of the most important elements a company can have. It is so powerful that it must be based on solid moral and ethical standards.

When I served in Viet Nam, I saw what great belief can accomplish. The Viet Cong are physically small and had primitive weapons. The U.S. definitely had a competitive edge in product and price. We had superior weapons, the best professionally trained soldiers, advanced technology, devastating air power and a well thought-out strategic plan. So what happened? They kicked our butts. Many claim it was the politicians' fault we lost. While that's a big part of it, I think a big reason was the Viet Cong's belief. They knew what they were fighting for. Most of our soldiers did not.

Mike Wallace interviewed a decorated North Viet Nam Colonel well after the war and asked him if he ever thought they would lose. The Colonel said that losing never crossed his mind. He went on to say that the Americans had such advanced weapons that he did not know how long it would take to win, but losing was not an option. It was his country, and he had great belief that their cause was right. Believing you are right is the key element in strong belief.

A strong customer-focused culture is a key cornerstone in building corporate belief. It is founded on correct moral and ethical principles. The philosophy of the culture is based on treating all customers with great respect. If everyone in the company treats customers, peers and vendors with great respect, belief must increase. Everyone in the company is responsible for their environment, from the CEO to the floor sweeper. Management must be the role model and monitor the system to insure execution.

When everyone in your company believes in the customer-focused philosophy and takes responsibility to insure the environment, belief increases. If that belief is founded on strong moral and ethical principles, your company becomes a force to be reckoned with. The employees are confident in the philosophy of their company.

Attitude

Most of your personal characteristics, such as enthusiasm, discipline, accountability, consistency and teachability are all enhanced by a great attitude. Being courteous and respectful at an early age will help you achieve great success later in life. No one likes to be around rude, foul, inconsiderate people. Let your peers see who you really are. Let them see a great attitude.

And remember, attitude is a choice, as easy to alter as putting on a smile. Simply decide to have a great attitude and – Voila! – you've got one.

Superior attitude was always the most important trait I looked for when hiring. When interviewing a potential employee, I would call their former clients to uncover their attitude.

> **Your attitude will determine your future.**

If there was any signs of a poor attitude, it would negatively affect the outcome of the interview. Your attitude will determine your future.

Attitude affects everything. A good attitude will allow you to learn more and work better with others. I do a simple exercise in my sessions in which the group lists all the characteristics of the ideal employee. It is an audience participation exercise and there is usually a long list that includes the following:

- Good listener
- Knowledgeable
- Aggressive
- Confident
- Good communicator
- Teachable
- Intelligent

- Caring
- Team player
- Belief
- Accountability
- Enthusiastic
- Disciplined
- Consistent

This list can go on and on, but it's basically the group's idea of the ideal employee. These characteristics would enable this employee to succeed in any job. Ninety percent of these characteristics spring from a great attitude.

Attitude is everything.

Look at my son, Bryan. He's an extremely gifted reader. He read *War and Peace* and *Crime & Punishment* by the time he was 18 years old. He is very intelligent, yet he barely got through high school and did not finish college. He read everything but his schoolbooks. His attitude got in the way and would not allow him to increase his knowledge in school. Now don't get me wrong – I love my son Bryan and I think he's a great guy who will maximize his great talent as his attitude allows. He's also a prime example of how your attitude affects every characteristic on the list.

You cannot reach your full potential without a great attitude. Your skills will get you to third base. Attitude will get you home.

Knowledge is all about attitude. Bad attitude will stunt your growth more than anything else. A great attitude will attract people and help you build strong relationships. It will also help you increase your ability to learn.

Self Esteem

Self esteem is very important to personal growth and monitoring success. People with self-confidence attract people with self-confidence. Knowing that you are not perfect is an important step. You must have strong moral and ethical beliefs. You take responsibility for your actions and confront and overcome your fears.

A strong customer-focused culture will help build self-esteem. Your company culture and management techniques are all based on sound moral and ethical principles.

Positive self-esteem is an essential part of your personal growth. Having confidence in who you are is very important. Unfortunately, we live in a world that seems to encourage emulating others – such as entertainers and athletes – instead of encouraging confidence in one's self. You gain nothing through idol worship. Many people who are idolized have very weak values.

The following insights can help you improve self-esteem.

1. Accept that you're not perfect. It is okay to be wrong and make a mistake. When you make a mistake and understand your mistake, then take time to correct and learn from it. That is growth.

2. Know that God doesn't make junk. We all have great talents. The challenge is in identifying them. Helen Keller, who was deaf, dumb and blind, wrote books. To develop our talents, we have to identify our strengths and focus on them daily.

3. Build strong relationships. Building moral and ethical relationships with moral and ethical people is very important. You will be like-minded in these relationships and inspire each other.

4. Take responsibility. Always examine yourself first in every situation. Identify what you could have done to make the situation better. It is a chance for you to find an area for improvement. Stop looking at other people's mistakes – you cannot change them. You can only change yourself. Do not get mad at yourself – remember you are not perfect.

5. Be true to yourself. Seek areas to improve. Do not lie and cheat anyone – and that includes yourself. When you identify an area where you are weak, confront it. If you are afraid to stand in front of a group and speak, for example, confront it by facing your fears. In our society, it is very important to be able to communicate one-on-one or in front of a group. There are many self-help books that deal with this, as well as college courses that can help. John F. Kennedy said, "Every man-made problem has a man-made solution." If you focus enough of your time in this area, you will find the solution.

Continual improvement is a sign of growth. Personal growth will improve your confidence and self-esteem. Spend your life doing the right things with the right people, always taking responsibility for your actions and life will be fruitful.

Quotes for Personal Growth

I like messages that are simple, powerful and memorable. These are some of my favorite quotes for personal growth. Remember – it is not what you hear, it is what you do.

"If everyone is thinking alike, no one is thinking at all."
General George Patton

"If you don't change your direction,
you will end up where you are headed."
Chinese Proverb

"Whether you think you can or whether you think you can't,
you are absolutely right."
Henry Ford

"Your attitude, not your aptitude, determines your altitude."
Zig Zeigler

"If it is to be – it is up to me."

"Do all the good you can, to all the people you can,
as long as ever you can."
John Wesley

"In the middle of difficulty lies opportunity."
Albert Einstein

"Rather to fail with honor than succeed by fraud."
Sophocles

"Anger is never without reason. But never a good one."
Benjamin Franklin

"Cleverness has never been associated with long delays."
Sun Tzu

"Knowledge is not power. The execution of knowledge is power."
Chuck Togias

"No one has a good enough memory to be a good liar."
Abe Lincoln

101

CHAPTER SEVEN

The Measure of Success

When people talk about someone being successful they always mention net worth. Making money is obviously very important, but it should only be considered an outcome of success, not the sole definition of it.

The true elements of success, as we will discuss in this section, are physical, mental and spiritual growth. Our being is comprised of body, mind and spirit. Imagine you have three plants in your home. If you only water two one will die. If you are taking care of yourself physically and mentally but not spiritually, that part of you will wither and die. When you have a daily regiment that focuses on all three elements, you are on your way to a happier – and more successful – life.

To stay strong physically you must exercise daily. When you do, you are healthier and happier. Your body will respond better and lessen your chances of a physical breakdown.

When you nourish your mind with substantial exercises, like meaningful reading and meditation, your mind starts to function better. I focus on material and authors that are morally and ethically sound. I want to learn, not just read.

Spiritual growth is also vital for your overall growth. When I mention this in seminars some people get nervous. It is almost like violating the separation between church and state. Yet it is a huge element of your success and well-being. Do not apologize for focusing on your spiritual growth. As I mentioned earlier, our politically correct society does not want anyone to stand for anything that could offend. Having these strong values based on a spiritual foundation will not only help you obtain success, it will separate you from the universal value system and that is good. Most people stand for a politically correct set of values, which is little more than having someone else determine your values.

When you are strong physically, mentally and spiritually, you are prepared to reap the rewards. You have self-confidence in your physical strength, the intelligence to compete mentally and a value system that will help you determine right from wrong. Grow and nourish your entire being, and you will be a formidable competitor in any arena.

Diversity of Thought

Gangs. What does that word make you think of? Evil, violence, murder, punks, thugs – these would all probably come to mind. But the other characteristic of gangs is that they absolutely lack diversity of thought. They dress alike, talk alike and think alike. This "gang" mentality prevents growth of any kind. If you were able to trace these gang members over the years, you would find that very few of them get out of that life - they never get the chance to reach their full potential. There's an old Chinese proverb that sums this up: "If you don't change your direction, you'll end up where you're headed."

In the inner city, if you speak out and disagree with the majority you are considered a traitor. I believe this is the number one reason that many people who live in the inner city never escape it. It certainly has nothing to do with talent – there is tremendous talent there. But there is little to no diversity of thought. "When everyone is thinking alike no one is thinking at all."

An indication of what can happen when there is little diversity of thought is Black America. Black Americans vote 90% Democratic. I find this very troubling.

> When everyone is thinking alike, no one is thinking at all.
> -- *General George Patton*

There has been no ethnic group or race in the history of this country that has ever voted as heavily in favor of one party. There are few leaders in the black community who encourage individual thought. Coincidently, Black Americans are at or near the bottom of the economic ladder. I feel most of their leadership has sold out lock, stock and barrel to the Democratic Party and because of that their economic situation has been negatively affected.

Strategically, it makes no sense whatsoever to put all of your eggs in one political basket. There's only one logical explanation I can come up with: the Republican party can now be used as a scapegoat if the plight of Black America does not improve. Sound harsh? Think about it. The Democratic "leaders" of the community will be able to accuse and condemn the Republicans, removing any and all blame from themselves and their lack of leadership. That only seems to makes sense if you never want to be accountable for your own actions.

If my conclusions are incorrect, and they may be, then I have no idea why their leadership would discourage diversity of thought. Don't get me wrong – I am not necessarily against the Democrats or for the Republicans in this case. I am against the leadership of an entire community discouraging diversity of thought among its constituents. When this happens, the community pays the price. The inner city is full of great talent, and encouraging diversity of thought could help maximize that talent.

Consider the reaction to Bill Cosby's remarks when he gave a speech at an NAACP gala in 2004 criticizing the parenting of lower-economic blacks. He was criticized for fueling negative racial stereotypes and giving credence to conservative beliefs that the problems facing African Americans are self-imposed. A few excerpts from Dr. Cosby's speech:

> "People marched and were hit in the face with rocks to get an education, and now we've got these knuckleheads walking around...The lower-economic people are not holding up their end in this deal. These people are not parenting. They are buying things for their kids--$500 sneakers, for what? And won't spend $200 for Hooked On Phonics. I can't even talk the way these people talk: 'Why you ain't, Where you is'... And I blamed the kid until I heard the mother talk. And then I heard the father talk. Everybody knows it's important to speak English except these knuckleheads. You can't be a doctor with that kind of crap coming out of your mouth."

Cosby then made a statement that I think holds true regardless of race, economic level, religion or anything else: "Racism continues to exist, but *there is nothing that will defeat parenting."* (Gets back to the 'great leadership begins in the home' discussion we had earlier in the book.)

So why was Cosby criticized so heavily? Why was he considered a traitor – and Uncle Tom – for giving his opinions? I am not a member of that community, so it's not for me to say whether he was right or wrong. But I do know that Bill Cosby is a very bright person and his opinions, whatever they are, should not be dismissed. They should be embraced and discussed. Good ideas on how to improve the lives of the community may result. The functional family is the model that successful sports teams, armies and communities follow. A strong family has a leader that encourages input from all, not just the members of the family that they agree with. Many opinions calmly discussed generate countless ideas and that is good. If Bill Cosby took the time to comment on anything I did, I would welcome his comments.

Many companies suffer the same way when they have strong dictatorial leaders. Diversity of thought is power. It is not bad – it is good. The most successful people I know always seek competent input before they make decisions. Not input from people who just agree with them, but rather people who do not agree with them. Whether you are in city leadership or corporate leadership, do not surround yourself with "yes" men. They are usually politically motivated non-thinkers.

The way you keep a group down is to not allow divergent thought. The key is being able to discuss the opinions civilly, which encourages differences of opinions. Remember, your place of work is not a talk show where the more people you have shouting over one another the better the ratings. Define the forum, bring in people with different opinions and discuss with a goal of resolution. The first few times it may be difficult, but after that, it gets easier and easier and the results get better and better.

Remember, diversity of thought is power.

Control Your Destiny
Good character is doing the right thing when no one is looking.

To control your destiny you must do a number of things. First, determine your real love. What career would you love to do for the rest of your life? If you won the lottery and could do anything you wanted, what would that be? When you're passionate about something, you have a very good chance to become successful at it. In addition, you have to understand the importance of building long-term relationships. Next find out all you can about your field of endeavor. Research your desired industry and its leading professionals. Explore what academic courses are needed to further your knowledge. Create a strong disciplined work ethic. Become a top professional in your industry, someone that stands out from all the rest through your knowledge and respectful treatment of customers.

Let me give you a good example of what happens when you learn to control your own destiny. Andy Boucounis is a friend of mine who owns a produce company. In case you didn't know (and why would you?), produce is one of the toughest businesses in America, fraught with early hours, high employee turnover, product spoilage and competitive price attacks. On top of all that, most in this business do not make a lot of money.

When Andy's father introduced him to the industry at a very young age, it was love at first sight. Andy's father taught him the business from the ground floor. Andy learned how to buy and sell produce effectively. He found out which distributors were best and always made them accountable for their product. Andy is very disciplined and has a strong work ethic and leads by example. He is very customer-focused to peers, vendors and customers. He treats his customers with great dignity and respect, and no

109

request is ever ignored. Peers are treated fairly and always praised and compensated for a job well done. Vendors are the truck drivers that deliver the produce, and they are also well respected and praised for a job well done by Andy.

The result of Andy's attitude is that he has very little employee turnover, his vendors love doing business with him, and he's become very successful in a very tough business.

Andy's reasons for success:

1. Passion for the business

2. Knowledge of the industry

3. Vendor accountability

4. Disciplined work ethic

5. Customer, peer and vendor focused.

So find what you love and control your own destiny. The results will astound you.

Humble Wins

Have you ever seen an NBA game where a player makes a great play and cuffs his hand behind his ear? The player is telling the crowd to cheer louder for his great accomplishment. You know what? For the million bucks a game he's making, *every* play had better be great.

In college football, a running back after scoring a touchdown poses in the end zone like the Heisman trophy. As coaches are fond of saying, "Act like you've scored before." I think a lot of this behavior dates back to Muhammad Ali, when he used to call himself "The Greatest." A little of that behavior goes a long way.

So it's no wonder fan enthusiasm for most pro sports is dwindling. Fans are getting sick of huge salaries and the behavior of these athletes. But some sports are actually on the rise. Golf and auto racing are becoming very popular with fans. I feel one of the biggest reasons is the behavior and mentality of these athletes.

Tiger Woods may be the greatest golfer of all time. He is very intense on winning every tournament. His golf shots are fantastic. Yet I have never seen him demean another player or showboat to get the crowd to cheer louder. When being interviewed he never sings his praises or ridicules another golfer. It is so easy to cheer for a Tiger Woods. The fans can embrace him because he demonstrates dignity and class. Most great golfers are humble and respectful and that, in my opinion, is why the game is flourishing.

In auto racing, the drivers are all associated with teams. Anytime they win, they know that their team was as responsible as they were in the victory. In the winner's circle the driver gives credit to his team members. How refreshing. Last I checked, baseball, basketball and football were team sports too. I think someone forgot to tell some of these other athletes.

To be fair, not all pro athletes are arrogant. I think Tim Duncan of the San Antonio Spurs is a great example. Duncan is the best power forward in basketball, but he never demonstrates arrogance. He never showboats or gestures to the crowd or tells people how great he is. He always gives his teammates credit and they in turn embrace him. The Spurs are a great team because of Tim Duncan.

In business as well as your personal life, if you want to build strong relationships with credible people, stay humble. Do not talk about yourself or your accomplishments all the time. When giving credit for something you have accomplished, always include those individuals who helped you succeed. Most importantly, do not take yourself too seriously. A friend once told me that the beginning of the end is when you start to believe all the nice things people say about you.

> There's no limit to how far a man can go when he gives others the credit.

You reap what you sow and you sow what you reap. People with class and character attract people with class and character. As an employer, employee, teammate or friend, be someone who your associates can be proud of. Give credit where credit is due, and be humble.

—

CHAPTER EIGHT

My Five Favorite Words

As you can probably guess from reading this book, I like simplicity. I am very black and white when it comes to life. I think the gray area is for someone who lost the debate and wants to justify his or her opinion. I admire anyone who can admit his or her mistakes. I like people who are morally and ethically strong.

As I said, I have an inclination for clarity and use a lot of quotes and powerful words. I think a word, when taken literally, can be very dynamic. My five favorite words can be remembered by the acronym ACTED:

- Accountable

- Consistent

- Teachable

- Enthusiastic

- Disciplined

We're going to examine each word so we can appreciate their meaning. We'll also demonstrate how each word is vital in a customer-focused environment.

Accountable

Being accountable for your actions shows great character. When you are accountable, you stand by your decisions and own up to them in spite of the outcome. If your decision was wrong, you will admit it and change direction. The best way to learn from your mistakes is to first admit you made a mistake. In a customer-focused environment, every member of the staff must be accountable to peers, vendors and customers in order for the system to be effective.

Recently, I was approached by a real estate company to discuss the possibility of training their staff with customer-focused techniques. I met with the sales manager, who previously worked for a large corporation, and was very competent in sales and management. She was hired by this real estate company to be the sales manager and trainer. Yet no one on the staff was accountable to her. They were, as she put it, independent business people and were self-employed. She even told me that she had a training session and only two out of thirty sales people attended.

I told her that I could not help her as long as there was no accountability. The owner who hired her put her in a position to fail. Which was too bad, because I think she was very qualified in sales techniques and would have helped the sales staff.

Accountability is a key to a successful company. You cannot have a customer-focused culture unless all employees are accountable. A company with a defined culture that is monitored for performance by management is going to be much more accountable to their clients. When the management and employees have created that culture, they will be even more accountable.

Consistent

You are what you continually do. Consistent behavior is predictable and important in building long-term relationships. I recently read a book on Abraham Lincoln who, because of his very strong convictions, was the epitome of consistency. He took over as President during arguably the worst time in American history.

Many Southern states had seceded from the union because of his election. The country was divided on the slavery issue, and civil war ensued. The Northern politicians thought Lincoln was dumb and weak, and the South hated him for his policies.

Friend and foe who interacted with Mr. Lincoln eventually gained great respect for him because of his consistent behavior. He always told the truth and never wavered from his stand on slavery. Everyone always knew where he stood on the issues. He was consistent in thought and deed.

In a customer-focused environment the way you treat a customer should always be consistent. Every customer should be treated with great respect. Consistency among staff is key to the success of a customer-focused culture.

Teachable

Someone who is teachable is always willing to learn. They are always looking for self-improvement. That is such an important characteristic in an employee. When I conduct seminars, I can usually tell who wants to be there. They sit up front, have a pen and pad, and ask many questions. They are there to learn. After the sessions, these same employees want my card and ask if they can continue to contact me. I always say yes because I love to talk to teachable people.

On the other hand, there are those employees who love to talk about how they've "paid their dues." What they are really saying is "I am not interested in learning anything new." How unfortunate. Many times these are older and more experienced employees who could be an asset to their company, if they only had a different attitude. If an employee is no longer teachable, they are replaceable. They should not be a member of a growing customer-focused company.

Sales people who are good listeners are trying to learn before they give a recommendation. The customer-focused salesperson must always be teachable because their philosophy is based on gathering information before selling.

When you are teachable, you listen to others and encourage input. You read books that pertain to your profession or your client's business. You want to be associated with cutting-edge companies that will challenge you.

Our lives will be enriched if we never stop learning.

Enthusiastic

This probably is my favorite of the five words. Enthusiasm truly is contagious. Every mission statement I help a client with has the word "enthusiastic" in it. I guess you could say it's my trademark. When you are enthusiastic in helping your clients, you have taken customer focus to the highest level. You will position you and your company above all others in your industry. When your company creates and monitors a culture that is focused on super serving each customer, your clients will profit. When each member of your company is enthusiastically committed to client, peer and vendor growth, your company and clients will achieve great success. I always feel good when I am with someone who is enthusiastically solving my problems. I know they really care.

As I said earlier, enthusiasm is contagious. Be enthusiastic about life and you will enjoy it more.

Disciplined

Being disciplined in your personal and professional life is usually very evident. People who are disciplined have a defined standard of living that refrains from over-indulgence. For example, people who are chain smokers are not very disciplined. All the data indicates that cigarettes are habit-forming and hazardous to your health; they will eventually kill you. A disciplined person could not be aware of the data and still smoke.

Another example is obesity. Overeating is a problem throughout our country. Why? Are people really that hungry? No, they just lack discipline.

Unfortunately, I could go on and on with examples of how people lack discipline. By contrast, disciplined people do almost everything in moderation. They also indulge in activities that are going to help them mentally, physically and spiritually.

When your company has created a customer-focused environment, it must support the environment with defined standards and disciplines. Each member of the staff will understand what good performance looks like and be monitored by management in its execution. Marines are a great fighting force because of their discipline.

Doing business without discipline is easy – simply let your employees define their own rules. But the result is usually chaotic for your customers. A well run customer-focused company has defined rules and regulations with disciplined employees who follow through.

Disciplined people have a vision for their lives, defined goals, correct procedures and a high success rate in their endeavors. Disciplined, well-organized companies enjoy the same success.

—

CHAPTER NINE

The Step2 System
HOW TO CREATE LOYAL CUSTOMERS IN AN UNLOYAL WORLD

As I mentioned in the Preface, this book is based on my Step2 Training System and my view of life. I have included this brief overview to explain the training process. The Step2 System is a series of building blocks that is specifically designed to motivate the creation of a customer-focused environment that is easy for management to implement and monitor. It is very clear and easy to understand, and can be implemented in most companies in a short period.

1. Creating Loyal Customers in an Unloyal World is segment #1. It focuses each member of your management and staff on the meaning of real customer focus. We will create a defined system that will astonish even the toughest customers and position each employee and company as a great value added resource. In these sessions, we will define our #1 job priority and true competitive edge. We will also define what each employee must do to live the system daily.

2. When the cultural training is completed, we start the Step2 Sales and Marketing sessions. In these sessions, we train sales representatives in techniques and terminology designed to maximize sales opportunities and position each representative as an important added value resource to their clients. This is all done within their new customer-focused culture.

3. After the company has become customer-focused and each representative has acquired the sales knowledge, we help management in the administrative area, formulating customer-focused job descriptions, training manuals and department plans. All designed to bring clarity and vision to each department.

There are two questions that you and your company must be able to answer when asked by a prospect:

    1. Why should I do business with your company?

    2. Why should I do business with you?

Many companies find these two questions difficult to answer because they do not have a defined corporate or individual identity.

Your customer has got to know how they will benefit when doing business with you. Most companies will lead with their product or price, and that is very dangerous. Product is a problem because most companies do not have products that are superior to their competitors'. Price is the weakest of all marketing positions because it can be compared and overcome so easily.

My Step2 System will help your company and employees create a defined identity. This identity will be very important in selling and retaining customers. We will also help create a system that reinforces your identity with proper procedures to ensure customer loyalty. Again the name of my seminars are "How to Create Loyal Customers in an Unloyal World."

To be effective, a training system should help each participant personally as well as professionally. My Step2 Training System is designed to focus on building relationships through your problem-solving abilities. When you are effective in building solid relationships, it will help you benefit in all areas of your life.

When the Step2 System is complete, your company will distinguish itself from your industry. Everyone in your company will become a dedicated problem solver. The system is sophisticated, yet simple and easy for departments to implement and management to monitor. In addition, because it's customer-focused, the system is subject to very little change.

I'm including here the Step2 Customer-Focused Questionnaire, which focuses on the company, corporate philosophy, competitive analysis, marketing information, selling philosophy, employee training and management. These questions are examples of what areas my company focuses on to help you become more customer-focused. You will notice at the end of each section there is a place for comments or recommendations. You do not gather information for the sake of gathering information. You gather information to give well thought-out recommendations to continually help grow and improve the client's situation.

The more you know about the client, the better opportunity you have to solve problems.

CLIENT NEEDS ANALYSIS

"I WILL NEVER ASK FOR YOUR BUSINESS UNLESS I CAN HELP IMPROVE YOUR BUSINESS"

Briefly describe your business._____
_____
_____
_____

COMPANY PHILOSOPHY

1   What is your company's #1 job priority?_____
_____
_____

2   Do you have a company mission statement?_____
   A If yes, who formulated the statement?_____
_____

   B Can everyone in your company recite your statement?_____
   C Is it driven by your customers?_____
   D Name 3 ways you demonstrate customer focus.
      1 _____
      2 _____
      3 _____

   E Define your customers:
      1 _____
      2 _____
      3 _____

3   Do your managers understand their #1 job priority?_____
   A Is it clearly defined?_____

4   Are your managers empowered to make decisions?_____

5   Are your employees empowered to make client decisions?_____
   A What does employee empowerment mean to you?_____
_____
_____

Comments:_____
_____
_____
_____

S·T·E·P
2
TRAINING SYSTEMS℠

124

CLIENT NEEDS ANALYSIS

COMPETITIVE ANALYSIS

1 List your 3 major competitors. _____

_____

_____

2 Do you have a defined competitive edge? _____

3 Versus your major competitor, how do you rate in these 3 areas?

Share of dollars _____

Product or services rendered _____

Employee training (expertise) _____

4 What are your company's major strengths? _____

_____

_____

A Major weaknesses? _____

_____

_____

5 What is your competitor's major strengths? _____

_____

_____

A Major weaknesses? _____

_____

_____

Comments _____

_____

_____

_____

_____

_____

S·T·E·P

TRAINING **2** SYSTEMS™

MARKETING INFORMATION

1 Who is your desired target?_____

_____

Age (heavy user) _____ Sex _____

Income _____ Location _____

Life Style characteristics _____

_____

_____

Socio-economic _____

2 What are your target's principle buying considerations?

1 _____

2 _____

3 _____

3 How is your company's philosophy conveyed to your target?

Radio_____ Billboards _____

TV_____ Trades _____

Newspaper _____ Other _____

4 Is the majority of your advertising tactical or strategic? (Please give

an example of your most recent ads)_____

_____

_____

5 Are you the market leader in your target's mind? _____

_____

Comments:_____

_____

_____

_____

S·T·E·P

2

T R A I N I N G   S Y S T E M S ℠

CLIENT NEEDS ANALYSIS

SELLING PHILOSOPHY

1 Do you have a Client Needs Analysis form?_____
(If yes, please show example.)

2 Does your CNA have only product-related questions?_____

3 Do your sales people share the CNA with other departments before
making client recommendations?_____

4 After CNA sessions do your sales people give their clients a choice
or specific recommendation?_____

5 Do your sales representatives understand the following about their client.
Buying cycle _____ Target _____
Target's buying consideration _____ Buying modes _____
Buying influences _____

6 Is it required that your sales reps keep updated, detailed client files?_____

7 Do you prioritize all your accounts (strategic account list management)?
_____

8 Is new business development important to your company's success?_____
A On a yearly basis, what percentage of your total business is new? _____

9 Do you have in place a new account development system? _____

10 What mode is your sales force operating in:
Creating demand or managing demand?_____

TRAINING

11 A Are your sales people trained in delighting customers? _____
B Are they required to know their mission statement? _____
C Do they have a list of added values important in creating customer
relationships? _____
D Do they have a list of standards and disciplines important in creating
delighted customers? _____
E Do they have PMR's? _____
F On a scale from 1 to 10, where is your sales force in customer
expertise? _____
_____

S·T·E·P
TRAINING **2** SYSTEMS℠

TRAINING (Continued)

12 How do your sales reps position themselves versus competitors? _____

_____

13 Have you developed a systematic approach to client problem solving?

_____

14 Sales department's greatest strengths? _____

_____

Weaknesses? _____

_____

15 Projections:

A Are they mandatory? _____

B Is an action plan submitted with projections? _____

C Who determines yearly projections (employees, manager or both)?

_____

D Are projections formulated account by account? _____

Comments: _____

_____

_____

_____

_____

_____

_____

MANAGEMENT SECTION

1 Do your managers submit departmental plans yearly? _____

2 Do your managers have written employee evaluations? _____

If yes, how many times per year? _____

3 Do your managers have a job description? _____

If yes, are supervisory and functional duties separated? _____

4 What are your managers' most important priorities? _____

S·T·E·P

TRAINING **2** SYSTEMS℠

128

MANAGEMENT SECTION (Continued)

5 Do your managers empower their employees? _____

6 What are your managers' greatest challenges this year? _____
_____
_____
_____

Comments: _____
_____
_____
_____
_____

CLIENT EXPECTATIONS

1 If you hire a consultant to help you improve your business, what

improvements are you expecting? _____
_____
_____
_____
_____
_____
_____

Comments _____
_____
_____
_____
_____
_____

S·T·E·P
2
T R A I N I N G   S Y S T E M S℠

ADDITIONAL QUESTIONS

1 What is the #1 reason for your company's success? _____

_____

_____

2 Where are your greatest growth opportunities? _____

_____

_____

3 Which department is your biggest money maker? _____

_____

_____

4 Do you have customer focus group sessions? With clients? _____

_____

5 Do you think it would be beneficial to develop a questionaire and give it to
your top 5 clients, to evaluate their perception of your customer focused
culture?_____

6 If there was one thing about your business that — if more people knew
about it — could bring you more business, what would that one thing be?

_____

_____

_____

_____

_____

Comments:_____

_____

_____

_____

_____

_____

S·T·E·P

2

TRAINING SYSTEMS℠

Afterword

Now, get out there and lead.

Well, you just read my view of the world as I see it; my thoughts on leadership, sales and self-improvement. Even though it should be fresh in your mind, I believe that lessons worth living are worth repeating. So I'd like to summarize the key points for you to remember as you close this book and begin becoming more successful.

Leadership

Leaders always define expectations and monitor results in a caring, disciplined environment. Great leaders are great people developers. In fact, the best way to recognize great leaders is to look at the corporation or communities they serve. If those entities are always improving, then that person is a great leader. Great leaders make everyone, including themselves, accountable for their actions. They think logically and plan strategically. They always look internally to solve problems, and they don't blame outside forces for which they have no control.

Sales

Great sales people are first and foremost great listeners. After all, information stimulates thought and leads to creative ideas that solve problems for the customer. Sales-people who immerse themselves in solving customers' needs will always be successful. This is reflected in the sales triangle on page 69 which, by the way, will never be outdated. You will always be a valuable resource to your customers when you solve their problems.

Self-improvement

Personal growth starts with a committed focus on improving yourself. The most crucial part of this is having a positive attitude. All the characteristics of the ideal employee (pg. 98) are enhanced with a positive attitude. Stop looking under a magnifying glass at others' shortcomings and look only to improve yourself. Greet people with a smile and a kind word and you'll immediately see and feel the difference. Pay special attention to improving your entire being: the mental, physical and spiritual.

When you improve in these areas, you will start to feel better about yourself and in turn will feel better about those around you. When making important decisions, get a lot of valuable input. Encourage diversity of thought – it is stimulating and will help improve your decision-making process. And always remember – in business as well as life, success only happens when you build strong relationships with uncompromising values.

I wish all my readers health and success. Thank you for reading my book. I am honored that you did so.

Chuck Togias

327148